TRAVELING HOPEFULLY

*How to Lose Your Family Baggage
and Jumpstart Your Life*

Libby Gill

With a Foreword by

Dr. Phil McGraw

St. Martin's Press 🞥 NEW YORK

www.stmartins.com

Design by Phil Mazzone

Library of Congress Cataloging-in-Publication Data

Gill, Libby.
    Traveling hopefully : how to lose your family baggage and jumpstart your life / Libby Gill. — 1st ed.
        p. cm.
    ISBN 0-312-32394-8
    EAN 978-0312-32394-3
    1. Self-actualization (Psychology) 2. Family — Psychological aspects.
    I. Title.

BF637.S4G487 2004
158 — dc22   2004046753

First Edition: October 2004

10   9   8   7   6   5   4   3   2   1

To the two best reasons for traveling hopefully,

my wonderful sons,

Harrison and Zach

Contents

FOREWORD BY

Dr. Phil McGraw

I talk a lot about accountability, about taking responsibility for your actions and your outcomes. It sounds simple enough, but understanding how the decisions we make create those outcomes in life is as profound a concept as I can imagine. In Libby Gill's *Traveling Hopefully: How to Lose Your Family Baggage and Jumpstart Your Life*, Libby brings that concept into crystal-clear focus for real people living in a real world. By having the insight and courage to take off the social mask and get real about the toxic family legacy that initially distorted her self-image, decision-making process, and approach to life, she has created an inspirational account of how she decided to lose her family baggage and reclaim her life. In a voice that is distinctly female, she challenges all of us to learn—and then change—how our past impacts our present and future. Bottom line: This book is for real because Libby is for real.

In my first book, *Life Strategies*, I laid out my personal ten laws of life. I didn't make these laws up, I simply observed the hard-and-fast rules of life that are there whether you like it or not. I did that to give readers a starting point for assessing what in their lives was working and what wasn't working. Only in awareness can you begin to affect positive change: You have to name it to claim it.

It was in my personal quest to claim that which I felt challenged to do that I met Libby Gill. I have always believed that in order to succeed you must create a nucleus of supporters who share your visions and your passions, and have the abilities to make important things happen. My vision was to use what skills I had to create a national platform of leadership in the ways of living in an ever-changing and demanding world. It immediately became evident that I needed a consummate professional, who shared my belief in an honest and results-based philosophy of managing life, to oversee and guide me as I navigated the slippery slope of the media world.

Enter Libby Gill! In fact, she was my very first hire on this new endeavor. I wanted someone who "got it" and realized we were about to break the model and do television the way it was supposed to be done. No Hollywood snob calling everyone "dahling" would cut it. The minute Libby walked in the door, I knew she was a down-to-earth straight-shooter with a good head on her shoulders. I was dead on. The fact that she'd "worked her way down the corporate ladder," as she called it, then quit her studio job to write a parenting book about stay-at-home dads, just made her more interesting.

I discovered that there was a whole lot more to the picture than had first met the eye. Although she appeared to be one of those people who just breezed through life getting pretty much whatever she wanted, that wasn't the case at all. What I learned was that Libby, like a lot of other real folks, had overcome a painful childhood colored by such family tragedies as molestation, suicide, and mental illness. Unlike so many who break under the strain, Libby had evolved into a loving mother and nationally respected professional. Despite that, she still carried enough of that family legacy to create a pattern of decision-making that resulted in a life that just didn't fit. She was making it work, but I sensed she was like the duck that seems to glide gracefully across the pond until you look just below the surface where the picture is one of chaos and turmoil. She knew it, too. Since then, I have watched Libby instinctively put all the Life Laws I talk about so often into action and reinvent her life.

By opening the door on the family skeletons and letting some light shine in, Libby discovered the powerful combination of internal clarity and external action that freed her from her past. She found the courage to leave a marriage that, despite best attempts, was not to be. She redoubled her efforts to build a new career around her true gifts, even to shed the unwanted pounds—and, seemingly, years—that held her back from her best physical health and well-being. Although it certainly was a lot to tackle in just a couple of years, Libby maintains that if she can do it, anyone can do it. It just takes a commitment to live by design and not by default.

Maybe that's why I've come to respect and appreciate her as a human being as much as I rely on her instincts and judgment as a professional. On the surface, we might not seem to have much in common, but in many ways, we speak different dialects of the same language. Everyone, including me, can learn from her journey. *Traveling Hopefully* is one adventure you don't want to miss.

Acknowledgments

I would like to offer thanks to the many people who have guided me through a lifetime of hopeful travels. First and forever, to my beloved boys, Zach and Harrison, who were so patient as they watched me write this book at my kitchen table: You are truly "the two best kids on the planet." To my mother, Barbara, and my siblings, Cecily, Bill, Ruth, and Cameron, I hope this book will bring us closer together in the present and future than we were able to be in the past. In loving memory of my father, Bill, and stepmother, Fran, whose lives were filled with so much sadness, I pray you are finally at peace. And my gratitude always to you, Ned, for your ever-patient nature and for loving our boys so much.

Having Phil and Robin McGraw in my life has been such an unexpected blessing. As individuals and as a loving couple, you are truly my role models for wisdom, kindness, and generosity.

A special thanks to my brilliant literary team: the amazingly talented Diane Reverand and all the wonderful folks at St. Martin's Press, the dynamic duo of Jan Miller and Shannon Miser-Marven, and the incredible staff at Dupree-Miller and Associates.

To Nancy Levine: I will be eternally grateful that you appeared as an answer to a fervent prayer and taught me that the universe is, indeed, a kind place.

As for my wonderful Support Squad of friends and colleagues who have inspired me with their expertise and loving guidance, a huge heartfelt thanks to you: Jan Landis, Wendy Winks, Sara Rutenberg, Sheila Feren Thurston and Rick Thurston, Lauren Levy, Vickie Sullivan, Andy Kaplan, John Wentworth, Manfred Westphal, Chandler Hayes, Louis DiCenzo, Michaela Starr, Mike Illig, Michelle Hair-Foti, Terry Meyer, Bridgett Walther, Joe LoCicero, Cameron Hutton, Cindy Bishop, Beth Metz, Laura Golden Bellotti, Lonnie Burstein, Pam Golum, Debra Thompson, Garry Corgiat, Christine Adzich, and Nancy Kaleel.

And, finally, to all my brave clients who have given me the great honor of helping them translate their dreams into realities: You are my passion and joy and I applaud you for your courage to travel hopefully!

Author's Note

What is history, but a fable agreed upon?
—Napoleon Bonaparte

The stories described in *Traveling Hopefully* were borne of personal experience and re-created from memory. The names of family members and mentors are real. The names and details about clients, former boyfriends, and others have been changed to protect their privacy and allow them to tell their stories when and how they see fit. If anyone depicted within these pages remembers circumstances differently, I welcome their comments and feedback. How better to encourage healing and rewrite legacies?

TRAVELING HOPEFULLY

1

Getting Past Your Past

*Understanding the Five Steps
to Jumpstart Your Life*

"To travel hopefully is a better thing than to arrive."
—**Robert Louis Stevenson**

I was my father's favorite. It would have been my oldest brother, David, but when he died I became not only the official middle child of the remaining five but also heir to Dad's affection, a limited, qualified affection, with many complex strings attached, although I didn't realize it until much later.

I always thought of my dad as sophisticated and charismatic, an accomplished psychiatrist and brilliant healer, a military doctor who seemed so authoritative and dashing in his dress whites with all his ribbons and medals, just like Gregory Peck in *Captain Newman, M.D.* As I sat by his hospital bed with my youngest son, Zach, who had insisted on coming with me to Tampa in case it was the last time he would see his ailing grandpa, I thought about how difficult it was for my father to use his gifts of caring and compassion for anyone in his own family, let alone himself. It took me years to comprehend fully that my father's emotional detachment colored my life and shaped my relationships, making me as desperate for love as I was sure that I didn't deserve it.

As I watched Dad drift in and out of sleep while Zach played with the new Beanie Baby we'd just bought at the gift shop, I realized that, though my father had been in and out of hospitals since I was a teenager, this time he would not be coming home. I read Zach his Beanie's "adoption papers" and burst into tears. It said on the tiny heart-shaped tag that the toy bear had been named Ariel for a little girl who'd died of AIDS at age seven, not much older than my son was then. I was overwhelmed by the pain and sadness; years of it came rushing to the surface as I held my sweet boy in my arms and tried not to frighten him with my tears. That's when I determined to change my father's legacy in those last days of his life, and in changing his, change my own.

As a veteran communications and public relations executive now running my own coaching and consulting firm, I was sought after as an expert in guiding my clients to identify and articulate what made them unique in their marketplace and then build a brand around it. My motto was "passion, planning, and perseverance," and recently I'd become more focused on working with individual and corporate clients to understand how their past affected their future, so they could determine if the energy they were expending was truly getting them where they wanted to go. Now here I was being put to my own test. As I sat by my father's bedside during his last days, I knew that as he was preparing to leave this life behind, I was beginning to build a new life.

My little one and I let Grandpa rest while we did what any heartsick mother and son would do—we rented a bumblebee yellow Mustang convertible and hit the road for an afternoon of alligator farms and amusement parks.

JUMPSTART YOUR LIFE

It took me a long time to realize how much of my personal story—that is, my beliefs about myself, my value system, and decision-making process—had been shaped by my family's story. Finally, at the age of forty, when I found the courage to admit that I was flat-out miserable and that the image of the successful professional I presented to the outside world had little relationship to who I was on the inside—I realized I had merely fulfilled a legacy designed by my family instead of by me. That insight was the first step in a profound process of self-healing that I've come to call "traveling hopefully."

Traveling hopefully is a way of moving through the world: the infinite number of decisions we make on a daily basis which, when woven together, form the pattern of our being. Sometimes we make our choices, large and small, based on a set of beliefs about ourselves that we didn't create, but rather accepted. When I recognized I was living a life built on the shaky foundation of my family legacy—my father's emotional distance, my mother's bitterness, my stepmother's mental illness—I understood that I had allowed my history to define my present and determine my future.

Once I accepted the fact that I was living a life that was more a reflection of that legacy than true to who I really was, I began the difficult but rewarding process of personal excavation. I began to strip away the façade that I'd been showing to the world for so long that it had become my reality, although it bore little resemblance to the real me. Only then did I begin to see myself as a living work in progress, a hopeful traveler intent on finding the purpose and the passion that would allow me to create the life I envisioned for myself. That process would allow me to write my own story—and to help you write yours.

Getting past your past and overcoming your family story so you can find your most joyful, passionate self isn't easy, but it is possible. There's an old expression: "The easy road often becomes hard, but the hard road often becomes easy." We're not going to take the easy road, but I'm going to make the hard road a little easier by showing you the Five Steps to Jumpstart Your Life. Jumpstarting your life is a process of intentionally designing a specific plan of action so you can envision and then actively create the life you want, instead of waiting around for it to happen.

Even if you're at the top of your game with a great job and a loving family, maybe you've heard that little nagging voice asking why you're working so much and enjoying it so little? Or why you wanted desperately to have children and yet have no time to spend with them? Or maybe you're just not sure anymore what would make you want to leap out of bed in the morning and tackle the day. I'm not saying that once you've conjured up a mental image of the life you want, that it will magically begin to materialize. Not at all. But once you understand what it means to jumpstart your life—in work, recreation, friendships, and family life—you can begin to remove the roadblocks that are keeping you stuck in place and start moving forward toward the life you want.

The Robert Louis Stevenson quote from which the title of this book is derived, "To travel hopefully is a better thing than to arrive," may well be the one lesson I took with me when I quit graduate school. I didn't take the master's degree in psychology I'd planned on. Hopeless, I lost all sense of direction and gave up. One of my professors had insisted that we all keep a book of meaningful quotes, and I had written down the

Stevenson quote in mine. I didn't understand its significance at the time, but something about the phrase "travel hopefully" resonated very powerfully for me then as it does now. As I began to search for the kind of life that would bring me a deep sense of satisfaction, the true meaning of that phrase slowly dawned on me. I came to realize that traveling hopefully is about moving forward despite whatever obstacles stand in your way, as you continually move toward a life that reflects your beliefs and values. The process itself, one foot in front of the other, and not the end result, constitutes the journey. I realized that I am the traveler and hope is my fuel.

The path eventually became clearer for me as I learned to ask the right questions: What was I most passionate about doing with my life? And how was I stopping myself from doing it? When I stuck to my path by focusing on these questions and looking for the answers, my life seemed to work. When I backslid, losing hope or succumbing to fear, moving forward toward the life I wanted became much more difficult. And as I started to share my story and the tools I'd created for myself out of desperation and a desire to change, I watched others put those tools to use and begin to rewrite their stories as well. That's how the Five Steps to Jumpstart Your Life came into being.

You might not have thought about your life as a story until now. Stop for a moment and consider how the major events and relationships in your past have shaped you. Can you see how those events have influenced your present and can continue to influence your future? Like it or not, you have written a story about yourself based on a set of assumptions you've either come to on your own or been handed by others. Your story is the sum total of the beliefs you hold about yourself.

Maybe your story is satisfying and positive and there are only a few aspects of it you'd like to rewrite. Or maybe, like

I did, you want to throw out the story you feel is perpetuating outmoded beliefs and values, and start from scratch: what kids on the playground would call a "do-over." For many years, my story was one filled with pain and loneliness. Finally, I made a conscious decision that there was a lot more to me than that and I was willing to make the necessary changes to rewrite my story to include greater portions of freedom, creativity, and passion. I still have my moments of pain and loneliness, but they no longer define my life.

As we work through these tools together, I'll provide you with concepts, broken down into written exercises and mental meditations, that embody the spirit of traveling hopefully and the process of jumpstarting your life. As you'll clearly see, all Five Steps are inextricably interwoven, yet require separate explanation so that you firmly grasp the concepts involved before you combine them.

THE FIVE STEPS TO JUMPSTART YOUR LIFE

- STEP ONE: DISSECT YOUR PAST SO YOU CAN DIRECT YOUR FUTURE

If you are living in denial about who you are and where you came from, it's going to be difficult to assess your current status and make the necessary changes to rewrite your future. Maybe you're the adult child of an alcoholic and have minimized your parent's addiction. Your reluctance to see the situation as it is, or as it once was, doesn't change those circumstances, it just makes it harder for you to figure out how they've shaped you and how you can begin to change. Or maybe you don't consider your childhood especially traumatic, but you remember all too well the sting of the little slights and offenses and have begun to comprehend how even those minor wounds taken to heart over a lifetime have left their scars.

- STEP TWO: LEARN TO LINK INTERNAL CLARITY WITH EXTERNAL ACTION

The potent combination of internal clarity and external action will be the cornerstone of your transformation. The problem is most of us do one without the other. We develop a heightened sense of internal awareness, what you might call trusting your gut or following your intuition, but don't act on it. Or just the opposite: Many of us are constantly on the go, but we haven't taken the time for the internal homework, so we don't really know where all that movement is supposed to take us. We're in motion for the sake of motion, like my son's pet mouse inside its little Plexiglas ball, just rolling around and bumping into the furniture. Once you learn to link internal clarity with external action, you'll have the insight to know where you want to go and the action steps to get you there.

- STEP THREE: RECRUIT A SUPPORT SQUAD

Is this all starting to sound a little trickier than you bargained for? Relax, you don't have to do it alone. If, like me, loneliness has long been a part of your personal story, you may be used to telling yourself that you have to do everything alone because:

- Nobody ever wants to help me
- I don't know where to turn for guidance
- I can't let anyone see how needy I am
- I can't trust anyone to do anything the way I would

Now let's rewrite that lonely story and imagine a life populated with generous folks who have your best interests at heart: your own personal Support Squad. Whether it's two people or twenty, it's much easier than you might think to create a support team to offer insight and inspiration, to help hold you accountable, and to celebrate your success.

- STEP FOUR: CREATE A TRAVELING HOPEFULLY PERSONAL ROAD MAP

Here's where the proverbial rubber meets the road on your hopeful travels. The first step has helped you understand how your family legacy has contributed to shaping the life you're living. The second step has shown you how to develop your internal clarity, then translate it to external action. The third step shows you the value of a support system and how you can establish a custom-made team to keep you motivated. This step guides you in creating a detailed road map with very specific, measurable goals to which you, or others, can hold you accountable.

- STEP FIVE: KEEP MOVING TOWARD WHAT YOU WANT AND AWAY FROM WHAT NO LONGER SERVES YOU

This positive momentum is the essence of hope—something you must never be without—because even in your most desperate, frustrating, or challenging times, you need to, as the old expression goes, "keep on keeping on." The fifth step will teach you what all winners know—that perseverance is everything—and show you how to make perseverance a habit.

It took me a lifetime to learn the lessons I'm about to share with you, but it doesn't have to take that long. In fact, you're beginning right this very minute. Traveling Hopefully is a process of shedding the outdated family legacy to which you've been clinging, consciously or not, and then replacing it with a level of awareness and self-compassion you might never have experienced before.

In addition to the Five Steps to Jumpstart Your Life, I have developed 21 Hopeful Tools to provide a framework for looking at life in ways that will guide you toward your goals. These philosophical concepts are reduced to exercises that will help you turn those ideas into action steps. Ideally, you should complete the exercise outlined within each Hopeful Tool before you go on to the next one, at least the first time through. After that, return to any exercise you want, whenever you want, to recharge your motivation. These tools are meant to keep you moving forward even when you're feeling frustrated.

As you read this book, I'll be asking you to do some deep thinking and intense soul-searching. Much like life itself, what you put in to this process will be directly proportional to what you get out of it. You may also want to start a Traveling Hopefully Daybook, a journal you can keep on your bedside table or carry with you, so that you can capture your thoughts and chart your progress while you work your way through the exercises described in each of the 21 Hopeful Tools. If you are concerned about tackling these exercises, not to worry. Just give them a try, there's no right or wrong. You might even surprise yourself at how quickly you get into the spirit of positive change.

DISSECTING YOUR PAST

Contrary to what you might think, given the premise of this book, rather than dwell on the past, I just want you to examine it. If you're not careful, you can get so caught up in your history that you neglect—or avoid—taking action steps toward your future. But looking back is a necessary starting point to moving ahead. So let's begin to deconstruct your past.

The first questions I want you to ask yourself are:

- Do I ever feel that I am hanging on to the emotional relics of my family legacy?
- Can I think of any negative messages from my childhood that continue to influence me, even though they hold me back from getting more of what I want out of life?

Just as a family inheritance might include stocks, an antique bracelet from a favorite aunt, or a mountain cabin where you vacationed as a child, a family legacy is the emotional inheritance that a family passes down from one generation to the next. Was your family life filled with love and laughter, leaving you a legacy of compassion and close relationships? Or was your family life marked by pain, illness, or cruelty, leaving a family legacy of worthlessness and fear of intimacy?

The bracelet from your aunt may become a cherished symbol of her love for you, while the mountain cabin where you endured childhood vacations filled with chaos and misery may be something to be disposed of. Emotional relics are a lot like that cabin. They are the negative aspects of the legacy you inherited from your family. You can either hang on to them or dispose of them. But you have to recognize them as the outdated and useless aftermath of your upbringing before you can loosen your grip on them. See if you're holding on to any of the following:

EMOTIONAL RELICS

Lack of confidence

Unsatisfying relationships

Lack of money and opportunity

Need for chaos and turmoil

Victim mentality

Sense of entitlement

Unwillingness to take risks

Need to control

Inability to trust others

When I had my midlife epiphany and began to acknowledge my deep desire to make the second half of my life significantly better than the first, it was as if I'd sent some kind of cosmic SOS out to the universe. Once I made the commitment and accepted the risk of bringing more passion and purpose into my life, the positive changes I envisioned began to materialize. I was astonished. I felt a little like Dorothy in *The Wizard of Oz*. I had had the power all along, I just didn't know it.

We'll be exploring Tool #1 and Tool #2 in this chapter to start you on the first step of dissecting your past so you can direct your future. If you answer the upcoming questions thoroughly and honestly, you will be able to inventory the emotional baggage you're carrying, then begin to unload it once and for all. Traveling Hopefully is not about blaming your flaws or disappointments on your parents or your grandparents or your siblings, and then running away from any responsibility. You can't change the past, and you can't control anyone's behavior but your own. What you can do is start to gain a healthy new perspective on your past by looking at the family messages that contributed to shaping your personality and your methods of decision-making. Once you begin to see some patterns emerge, you can decide if you are hanging on to baggage better left behind.

Naturally, families come in all shapes and sizes so even if I refer to parents, feel free to substitute the family members who fit as you assess your relationships and begin to identify the blocks that might be holding you back. Adjust your answers or the exercises themselves to fit your situation. In other words, don't get hung up on my language or the specifics of my family situation and especially don't use them as an excuse to reject the tools I'm offering you. You're reading this book for a reason, so let's face the past and embrace the future together.

Objectively dissecting the primary relationships in your life or critically examining your behavior and that of the family members who've had the most impact on you is not easy. Just remember, this has nothing to do with pointing fingers or assigning blame and everything to do with moving toward a more productive and powerful life. Chances are, you've already had some thoughts about how you're letting your history interfere with your present. Perhaps you'd like to invest in real estate but you hear your dad's critical voice in your head admonishing you that you don't know the first thing about money, and it stops you in your financial tracks every time. Or maybe Dad wasn't harshly critical, but so overprotective you've never learned to take a risk or trust your own judgment. Perhaps you pick romantic partners who re-create the chaos and instability of your childhood home, even though you're longing for a solid relationship based on trust and intimacy. So let's take a look at your legacy, and see who you really are underneath all that family baggage.

Tool # 1: Tagging Your Family Baggage

Cheryl was a client from a wealthy northern California family who was referred to me when she was undergoing a career transition. As soon as we started working together, it became clear that Cheryl wasn't really in career transition. She was in constant flux in both her career and her relationships, unable to identify anything or anyone that she could stick with for more than a few months. Now in her thirties, Cheryl was beginning to see how she had convinced herself that stability and security were to be avoided at all costs.

We began to create a vision of the kind of life that would bring Cheryl a sense of purpose, without sacrificing freedom. Bit by bit, it became clear that her family legacy of fearfulness and uncertainty, brought on by growing up with a clinically depressed mother and an overcontrolling father, had made Cheryl unable to trust her own instincts in her personal or professional life since her father had ruled the house with an iron fist in an attempt to compensate for his wife's inability to contribute. Although, thanks to therapy, Cheryl began to understand the concept of family legacy, she was still frustrated by her seeming inability to make significant changes in her life. As an adult, Cheryl continued to feel dependent on her father, and the other men who came into her life, but also resentful of any help they gave her. Eventually, as Cheryl realized how her family legacy had shaped specific decisions, or failure to make decisions, she began to risk taking the steps that would move her toward a more satisfying life.

In order to get the most out of each tool in this book, choose a comfortable and quiet place so you can clear your head and give some focused attention to your answers. If you'd like to start recording your answers on paper, designate a journal or notebook as your Traveling Hopefully Daybook. You can use your daybook to write out the exercises along with your answers, as well as your feelings and reactions to each tool. Much like fitness training or playing the piano, building the necessary skills to create the life you want requires effort and repetition. So still your mind and quiet your body, then answer these ten questions as candidly as you can.

EXERCISE: THE FAMILY BAGGAGE QUESTIONNAIRE

Respond yes or no to each of these questions.

1. Do you think you would be leading a dramatically different life if your parents had been more supportive or nurturing?

2. Do you ever fantasize about the kind of family in which you would like to have grown up?

3. If you are a parent yourself, do you think of specific ways you can parent your children differently than your parents parented you?

4. Do you still talk to your parents in a manner similar to how you did when you were a child or adolescent?

5. Do you ever wish you had better relationships with your siblings or extended family?

6. Do you have personality traits that you find unattractive in yourself that you believe were a direct result of your upbringing? Like the emotional relics we've already discussed, do you think you are overcontrolling, distrustful, etc., as a result of your family legacy?

7. Do you ever feel "I'm becoming my mother" or "I'm just like Dad"?

8. Do you think you've inherited negative tendencies that may go back beyond your parents or even your grandparents; for example, a violent temper or a lack of motivation?

9. Do you ever wish you could turn off the sound of your mother's or father's voice in your head telling you what to do, what not to do, or how to live?

10. Do you feel that the good qualities you've developed were in spite of rather than because of your upbringing?

If you answered yes to five or more of these questions, you might want to run that baggage through an X-ray machine to take a closer look at what's inside. Most of us believe we've picked up negative self-images from our family that range from uncomfortable to toxic to debilitating.

Gregory was the son of a first-generation Polish immigrant mother and a wealthy merchant father. Throughout his life, Gregory received mixed messages from his parents about everything from social status to sex to education. Gregory's mother was frequently dismissed by others as a woman who had married far above her class because she was beautiful, and very possibly pregnant when she married. Gregory's father was considered the benevolent benefactor who had rescued her from a life of impending poverty, and he did little to dispel that myth. In truth, Gregory's father was harsh and cold to his wife, and to Gregory and his two sisters, while his mother was warm and loving. But because of his father's judgmental attitude toward his mother's immigrant status and broken English, Gregory grew up in humiliation, feeling inadequate to protect his mother and unworthy of his father's affection. He remembers the names his father called him in English and in Polish, as further degradation, and how those names have stayed with him for a lifetime.

Though our parents may have initially hung those un-wanted tags on us, we're the ones who have incorporated them into our personalities. We can make the decision to jettison them. First, it'll help if we identify those family messages by doing what I call "tagging your baggage."

EXERCISE: TAG YOUR BAGGAGE

Take a look at the following list and tag any description, by noting the word or phrase in your daybook or on a separate piece of paper, that represents a label you believe your family gave you. Add any additional labels, including those double-edged family nicknames, to the list as well. For now, we're only looking for negatives. We'll turn to the positives in just a minute.

Picky

Mean

Self-involved

Sissy

Aggressive

Angry

Stupid

Stingy

Unfriendly

Loner

Sad

Moody

Scared

Impossible to get along with

Lazy

Smart-aleck

Loser

Hyper

Talkative

Ugly

Skinny

Slow

Mama's boy

Lousy at sports

Fat or chubby

Never amount to anything

Clumsy

Spoiled

Crybaby

Bitchy

Loud

Reckless

Slutty

Untalented

Timid

Selfish

Temperamental

Controlling

Bratty

Clumsy

Needy

Crazy

Undisciplined

Shy

Manipulative

Sloppy

Useless

Pathetic

Bossy

Show-off

How many labels did you tag? Do you remember your family attributing these qualities to you when you were a child or adolescent? How did being called these things make you feel then? Do some of these labels still get a rise out of you today?

Thinking back through all those family baggage tags is a powerful experience. When I go through this list and tag my baggage, I find nine labels that were attributed to me as a kid, including "bossy," "picky," "show-off," and "talkative."

Let's sort through that baggage and see if we think the labels were really accurate or not. Go back to your list and next to each tagged bag write "Accept" or "Reject," meaning you agree or disagree with that label. As you're accepting or rejecting your baggage, note your emotional reactions and if any of these tags are particularly painful for you, even now.

Put an X to indicate whether you accept or reject each tag. My list looked like this:

MY TAGS	ACCEPT	REJECT	MY EMOTIONAL REACTIONS
Picky		X	Misunderstood and unfairly judged
Moody		X	Who doesn't have moods?
Smart-aleck	X		
Talkative	X		
Chubby	X		Always felt fat even when I wasn't
Spoiled		X	Still feels unfair to me
Loud	X		
Bossy		X	This trait should have been cultivated
Show-off	X		
Bratty		X	I was less bratty than most kids
Manipulative	X		

Even as I rejected some of my tags as being inaccurate and not reflective of who I was as a child and who I am now, I could still feel the power they held over me. It's as if I still feel the need to convince my family that I wasn't picky and spoiled, just discriminating. I wasn't a bossy show-off, but a child who was aching to be recognized for her creative talents.

When I thought more deeply about the labels I had been saddled with, I realized some were half-truths. For example, my picky, bossy, show-off tag was half true because I was an expressive, boisterous kid who loved to be the center of attention. When my natural exuberance and flair for drama was negatively characterized as picky, bossy, or show-off behavior, I accepted the half-truth of these labels as absolutes.

I learned to be ashamed of my desire to live a creative life and for years supported other artists, while secretly longing to act or write or dance.

Maybe your labels don't reflect the truth at all. If your parents slapped you with baggage like "stupid" or "crazy" or "crybaby" when they were the ones who were abusive and out of control, the sting of that abuse can last a lifetime, especially if they also told you they loved you, or you should respect them, or they were the only ones who would ever look after you. You were little, and they were big. More important, they were your parents, so you believed all their negative stories and, eventually, those stories became you. But you're not a kid anymore. You can handle any negative emotions that might arise as you dissect your past in order to rewrite your future.

REWRITING MY FATHER'S LEGACY

Sometimes the baggage we're given by our families lies not in what is said, but what is unsaid. In absence of verbal expression from our parents about their love for us, we interpret their actions or their emotions to write our own stories. Sometimes our interpretations are accurate, often they are not. I was ten when my parents' marriage ended and I gained the then-rare distinction of being the only kid in my class from a one-parent home. For the first two years of their separation, my father lived about an hour's distance from us and saw the kids on alternate weekends. When he remarried two years later, he and his new family moved across the country to Washington state. Two years after that, they moved across the Pacific to Japan, where I would eventually join them.

Through all those unsettling changes, my parents said little about the dissolution of their marriage or their feelings for us.

We were left to form our own conclusions. In my case, I wove my father's stoic silences into a story of my never being good enough or smart enough to please him. In my young, unformed mind, that was why he moved far away from me without offering any consolation or even explanation. I would never be worthy of his attention.

A couple of weeks after my son and I made that visit to my dad in the hospital, I returned to Tampa to see him again, this time by myself. My son had said his good-byes, now it would be my turn. My brother Cameron, who had also gotten the panic call from the hospital, was en route from Jacksonville with his wife, Zizi. Since my other three siblings hadn't spoken to my dad in at least two decades, we didn't expect them to start now.

As I braced myself for an emotional farewell to my father, I had a jolt of internal clarity: This would be the last time for me to say whatever it was I needed to say. I'd recently begun my hopeful travels, starting with quitting my corporate job so I could write a parenting book about stay-at-home dads, but I still had a very long way to go to unlearn the negative lessons of my childhood, some taught to me by my mother's harshness, some by my father's distance. When I linked my parents' messages, they became lessons like "don't bother speaking up, because no one is listening and no one cares" and "you might as well put other people's needs, goals, and dreams ahead of yours because yours don't count." If I wanted to take a step toward reversing my legacy of feeling discounted and unheard, I'd have to speak up—and soon.

I arrived at the hospital and was informed by the nurses that I was my father's medical surrogate, meaning I would be expected to make all decisions on his behalf, including, quite literally, the life-or-death measures. My father, who rarely shared his personal life or his feelings, had not told me about this last task nor did we even once discuss how he wanted his affairs handled. After spending some time with my father, who was heavily sedated, on a respirator, and unable to speak, Cameron, Zizi, and I headed for Dad's apartment to see what his paperwork might tell us about his last wishes.

We discovered that Dad did not want to have any extraordinary measures taken to keep him alive, meaning he didn't want to stay on life support. What we needed to do was clear. Although the hospital staff tried to talk us into leaving Dad on the respirator indefinitely, we knew that was not what he wanted. Not that we'd really needed the paperwork to tell us that.

Still, this was a big decision; although Cameron shared it with me, I was older and legally responsible so I felt the full weight of what I was doing when I told the doctors to remove the breathing apparatus. They seemed a little surprised, expecting the decision to have taken us a couple of days, instead of a couple of hours. There was no debate involved. It was what he wanted, it was what we wanted for him, it was what we would have wanted for ourselves. And so my brother and I instructed the staff to turn off all the equipment. A very kind nurse pulled me aside to tell me that hospitals generally preferred terminal patients to die without disconnecting their life support, hinting that it made things less sticky for them legally, but that I was doing the right thing. I appreciated her support, though I didn't really have any doubts. I knew what I needed to do for him. And for me.

I stood by Dad's bed and told him what would happen and how he would feel when the tubes that were breathing for him were removed. He was a physician and, had he been conscious, he would have been much more aware than I that his systems were about to shut down, one by one, until his lungs and heart stopped working. The doctors told me he was so heavily medicated that he couldn't hear me, but I knew better. When I told him that I would be by his side, holding his hand and talking him through his death, his eyes fluttered open and he squeezed my hand with what was probably the last bit of strength in his body. I had the strangest sensation that it was as if he were seeing me clearly, really seeing the woman I had become, for the very first time.

I proceeded to tell him all the things I'd never had the courage to say, that I loved him and that I knew how much he loved me, even though he'd never told me. I understood that it had always been difficult for him to express his feelings for me, or anyone else as far as I knew, but that I knew he was proud of me and all I had accomplished with my family and my work. It was a one-sided conversation, but one of the most honest we'd ever had. I suddenly felt the weight of the world rise off my shoulders, or maybe it was my dad's energy rising up to seek a better place than he'd ever found on earth.

Tool # 2: Unloading the Family Baggage

Telling my dad what I longed to hear him say, even though he'd never said it and was no longer capable of it, was almost as good as if he'd said it himself. My father was not an easy man to connect with. Of all his children, I think I had tried the hardest to make that connection. The fact that we shared a love of travel and books made us appear closer, but his love for me was an intellectual love. For most of my life my father had been geographically distant, living on the West Coast when I was in the East and on the East Coast when I was in the West. For all of it, he'd been emotionally distant. All my life, I'd felt unlovable and unworthy in my father's eyes. I finally spoke up at his deathbed. My conscious act of fulfilling a lifelong need to be heard by my father was a profound experience. It was as if

I had rewritten the slate. Rather than being the kid whose high school graduation and college plays weren't worth attending, I was finally loveable, worth listening to, important, all the things I'd never believed about myself.

I began to apply that same sort of flip-side logic to the rest of my family baggage tags. I thought about how my mother considered me picky. Rather than seeing myself as picky, I realized I was discerning and had a great sense of style. Wow, that felt a lot better. When my then-husband referred to me as "the malcontent," because of my relentless drive and dissatisfaction with the status quo, I just flipped the tag over to its positive side and began to think of myself as highly motivated, or when I was feeling especially chipper, visionary. Again, a much better fit. I just took the half-truth and balanced it with qualities that were positive and inspirational. It astounded me that something so simple could make me feel so much better.

EXERCISE: APPLYING FLIP-SIDE LOGIC TO YOUR
FAMILY BAGGAGE

So let's apply Tool #2 to your family baggage. Here's what I want you to do. Take another look at your list of negative descriptions, your tagged baggage. Now, I want you to rewrite each of those labels with something that is accurate and reflective of who you are today, but is at the same time energizing and positive. Label the old tags "Negative Tags" and label the new ones "Positive Tags." Doesn't that feel better already?

My list looks like this:

NEGATIVE TAGS	FLIP-SIDE LOGIC TO: POSITIVE TAGS
Picky	Discriminating, great taste
Moody	Sensitive, compassionate

Smart-aleck	Irreverent, flair for irony
Talkative	Great communicator
Chubby	Fit, curvy
Spoiled	Knows what she wants
Loud	Articulate, zest for life
Bossy	Strong leader
Show-off	Born entertainer, fun
Bratty	Little girl with big attitude
Manipulative	CEO material

If you're not used to looking at yourself in a positive light, and many of us aren't, you may be concerned that you've gone a little bit overboard and that you might not be, well, all that. So why not enlist a trusted friend or family member for a reality check and alternate perspective? Let them complete this exercise—as you. See what they come up with and if it corresponds with your thinking about yourself. Sometimes we think we know how others see us, but going down a checklist leaves little to the imagination. You'll know for certain just where they stand with regard to your family tags. Just make sure you choose someone whom you genuinely trust to have your best interests at heart so you end up on the positive side of your baggage!

SUMMARY: A SINGLE STEP

An old saying has it that even a journey of a thousand miles begins with a single step. Congratulations. You've just taken the first step toward Traveling Hopefully by completing chapter one of this book. You've learned about the Five Steps to Jumpstart Your Life and seen how you can integrate those concepts into your journey. You've also begun to work your way through the 21 Hopeful Tools, which will give you greater understanding and mastery of the process of defining, refining, and structuring the kind of life you want to live, step by step.

Just remember that determining the kind of life you want and then figuring out how to go out and get it is not an easy, or overnight, process. So keep the faith and forgive yourself each time you backslide. Like any new skill, traveling hopefully takes practice and patience. In chapter two, we'll examine the childhood dramas we've allowed to metastasize into ongoing negative stories and identify the obstacles we've built based upon those stories. Then we'll explore our happiest dreams and memories of childhood to see if that youthful exuberance holds lessons for us today as we continue to dissect our past to rewrite our future.

2

Don't Push the River, It Flows by Itself

Dissect Your Past to Direct Your Future

"We must accept finite disappointment,
but we must never lose infinite hope."
—Martin Luther King, Jr.

The St. Johns River flowed north, like the Nile, through the little town of Mandarin, Florida, just outside Jacksonville, the state's northeasternmost city. The river was beautiful but could be treacherous, concealing cottonmouths, moccasins, and even an occasional gator. As one of six children, I learned early on to read the nuances of the river that bordered our young lives, looking always for signs of trouble.

In this chapter, you'll continue to explore the First Step to Jumpstart Your Life as you dissect your past more deeply in order to rewrite your future. As we saw in chapter one, the Hopeful Tools are designed to help you change the way you think about your life. With Hopeful Tool #3 you'll examine the most dramatic and traumatic experiences of your childhood, then deconstruct your feelings about those events so that you can begin to transcend your negative stories. With Hopeful Tool #4, you'll revisit your fondest childhood dreams and reclaim some of the youthful zest you may have left behind so you can bring a sense of wonder and adventure back into your life today.

When I look at my past, one of my most vivid memories is of my childhood home and what it meant as a symbol in my family's story. Our family's house on the riverfront in Mandarin was a wondrous thing, especially in memory, where it looms much larger, more intricately detailed and laced with Southern charm than, perhaps, would register now through my adult eyes. Our house, which was built on land that once belonged to Harriet Beecher Stowe of *Uncle Tom's Cabin* fame, was one of those traditional Southern beauties made of sturdy white clapboard softened with forest green shutters designed to blot out the devastating midday sun.

With six bedrooms, four fireplaces, a library as well as roomy living and dining rooms, and an old-fashioned kitchen with a butler's pantry and back service porch, it was plenty spacious for our big brood. In addition to the tennis court and swimming pool—luxury add-ons by my parents—and the ten-acre horse pasture just down the road, it had a few of those mysterious antebellum touches we loved, including a hidden staircase that pulled down out of the master bedroom ceiling, an attic that ran the length of the house, and a basement with coal chute still intact. There were even a couple of outbuildings and a garage with a dangerous-looking mechanic's pit in the ground and servant's quarters up above.

Mandarin, now just another subdivision with the distinction of a prime riverside location, was then considered an upscale rural community, where people owned horses and lived on sprawling grounds studded with oak trees and azalea hedges. Though few ranched anymore, most people still had cattle guards made of slatted metal grates laid over the ends of their long driveways. There were horse troughs at intervals down the tree-lined center island of Mandarin Road, the town's main thoroughfare. We even picked up our mail every day at Miss Aggie's General Store, where you could still buy penny candy while you visited with Aggie, a white-haired grandmotherly type right out of central casting.

This was the mid sixties; we were supposedly on our way to a more enlightened era, but there were still many remnants of that old Southern way of life evident throughout our little neighborhood, the alluringly lazy gentility as well as the cruel slap of segregation. Orange Picker Road, just on the other side of Mandarin, was the dividing line between the rich white families, with their riding stables and long wooden docks that stretched out into the St. Johns, and the poor black families, with broken-down washing machines and rusted-out cars mounted on concrete blocks in their front yards.

We noticed all that when we were kids, but it was just one of the many things that weren't to be discussed or questioned. There were numerous topics that were taboo, off limits for discussion, when I was a child. Sometimes the silence was imposed by society, but more often by my parents' discomfort at dealing with difficult issues and deep emotions. That inability or unwillingness to acknowledge my feelings or share their own made the dramas of my childhood even more traumatic than they needed to be.

One unforgettable day when I was ten years old began with my being the first to awaken on Christmas Day. With six kids, you can imagine how loud Christmas morning usually was. Just a regular day would often hit decibel levels that could cause permanent hearing loss. That December 25, I awoke to a strange stillness. The ominous silence was so weighty it felt almost like a fog rising off the river just beyond the back porch.

By the time I reached the kitchen, Cecily and Ruth had joined me. Billy and Cam were trailing along just behind.

When we all piled into the kitchen, we discovered Mrs. Rahn, our neighbor from down the street, sitting at our big round table. On those rare occasions when Dad was home before dark and had dinner with the family, we'd eat in the dining room. The rest of the time, the kitchen was the province of us kids. My mother had had the oversize table built out of oak and bolted to the floor. We'd eat our chili mac or Chef Boyardee ravioli and pretend we were sitting at our version of King Arthur's Round Table, giving each other names like Sir Laughs-a-lot or Queen Vinegar.

The first thing that struck me as odd was not that Mrs. Rahn was sitting at our round table on Christmas morning instead of in her house down past County Dock Road, even though we rarely saw grown-ups sitting in our kitchen. It was that she was drinking coffee, something neither of my parents ever did.

And now, here was Mrs. Rahn sitting at our table, drinking coffee, and looking at us in such a way that we knew something terrible had happened. "David's been in an accident," she told us. "Your mom and dad are in the emergency room at Baptist Hospital with him now." She stood up — I couldn't tell if she would try to hug us or if she just wanted a refill. And then a sob broke from my guts so loud I can still feel it today.

David was the oldest of the six and had just come home on holiday break from his freshman year at Princeton. He was smart and handsome in his white tennis sweaters with the little rim of burgundy around the V-neck. His girlfriends were prettier than Annette Funicello, and everyone thought he would be a successful doctor or lawyer.

The others were all crying now, too. Even though Mrs. Rahn had a bunch of children of her own, she didn't seem to

know what to do. One of us, Cecily I think, asked her what
had happened. She told us that David's friend's VW bug had
spun out of control on Beauclerc Road when David and his
friend John were coming home from a Christmas Eve
party. John, who was the passenger, was shaken up but
not badly hurt. David had been thrown from the car and hit
his head.

It sounded really bad. I thought of the necktie under the
Christmas tree that was to be my big brother's present, a yellow paisley pattern that I thought had just the right touch of
sophistication for a college man. I wondered how I would
ever bring myself to look at that little package wrapped in its
sad, shiny foil.

My parents had intended our home to be a haven, a privileged country life of prep schools, Ivy League colleges, country clubs, and cotillions. They never anticipated the drama
that would unfold, shattering their dreams, and ours, with the
events set in motion that Christmas. David died that morning. For years, my mother consoled herself by boasting that
the church at which the memorial service was held was so
jam-packed that the overflow crowd had to stand outside on
the front steps. Less than six months later, my parents' marriage became the second casualty in my life, though far from
the last.

Tool # 3: Deconstructing Your Childhood Dramas

Like my experience of losing my brother, particular moments from our childhood are indelibly etched into our psy-
ches. Catalogued like mental snapshots, the images are frozen
in time and often incredibly detailed in our mind's eye, even
when we wish we could forget them. Some of these events are
truly traumatic, like the tragedy of my brother's death. Other

experiences may be more dramatic than traumatic, but even the small dramas that are not so deeply significant can leave their mark.

Maybe you vividly recall the pain you felt at the death of a beloved pet, the awkwardness of being the new kid at school, or the humiliation of putting an intoxicated parent to bed. Most of us also have other, happier, childhood memories like the thrill of winning a track meet or the pride of hearing an audience applaud your solo in the school concert. What stands out among our childhood memories can span the entire spectrum of human emotion from darkly tragic to ridiculously trivial. Even though many of us share common experiences, in our minds each snapshot captures a moment that is uniquely personal and specific only to us.

Often it's not the event that is truly significant. What is significant about each of these highlights and lowlights of childhood aren't the circumstances themselves or even how high the highs or how low the lows. What is key is how you interpret and internalize—and sometimes magnify—those childhood dramas, allowing them to shape who you are today.

Susan is a successful attorney specializing in entertainment law. She is considered a top-notch lawyer, a great mom, and a loving friend by people in her social and professional circles, yet often views herself as the fat girl whom no one likes. When we discussed childhood dramas, she admitted that she was still haunted by the memory of her tenth birthday party. It was a slumber party to which she had invited twenty girls and only two showed up. Susan was mortified and admitted that even today when she takes the risk to reach out to people beyond her closest inner circle, she expects to be rejected just like she was when those eighteen girls declined her invitation. Granted, lots of children experience that kind of rejection, but Susan had not only hung on to the experience but allowed it to fester in her memory, causing even more pain and disappointment now than it had then.

Everyone experiences childhood dramas, from striking out in the ninth inning to their parents' divorce. But do you allow that strikeout to make you feel like a loser or the divorce of your parents to shape your belief that members of the opposite sex are not to be trusted? We'll examine events that represent that spectrum of childhood dramas from trivial to tragic. See if you recognize yourself in any of these negative scenarios. See if can remember how these events made you feel at the time and if you may have magnified them in your memory, making them even more devastating than they were at the time. In a moment, we'll look a little more deeply at how you can begin to let go of some of the pain and power you've attached to those memories.

CHILDHOOD DRAMAS

How have you written your stories of childhood? And how can you rewrite them now to give them the kinds of endings you've always wanted? Have you immortalized your personal childhood dramas into stories that empower you or make you a prisoner of your own memories? Have you allowed your stories to enslave you, making it impossible for you to overcome the negative messages? Or have you learned to trump the hand that life has dealt you? We've all heard stories like the one about the two brothers who grow up in the same abusive household, yet one becomes a successful entrepreneur and philanthropist while the other becomes a drunken derelict. What does the successful brother know that the derelict does not? And how do we live our lives to follow the successful brother's example? In other words, how do we process the negative experiences from our childhood so rather than becoming roadblocks and deterrents to our happiness, they become inspiration for change?

Deconstructing your childhood dramas is a way of putting some realistic and appropriate perspective on the events of your past. This process of examining past traumas, even the minor ones, will allow you to let go of the negative emotions and the resulting roadblocks you've built as defense mechanisms to deal with the pain. Those defenses may have allowed you to get through the drama of the moment, but often you hold on to that defensiveness far beyond its usefulness. Now, that once-useful mechanism is simply holding you back from creating the life you want.

In my case, I held on to the pain of my brother's death rather than grieving my loss. I was unequipped at age ten to manage my own feelings and had nowhere to turn for guidance. Consequently, David's death took on a sort of mythic proportion as a negative turning point, the beginning of my family's demise. Since my parents rarely discussed the circumstances or emotions surrounding my brother's passing, the lesson I took away was that it was better to attempt to shut out the pain than deal with it. What I didn't understand until much later was that shutting out pain also meant shutting out a lot of positive emotions as well. As I continue to unfold my story throughout this book, you'll see how I let my roadblocks, primarily my fears of vulnerability and risk, systematically rob me of the life I wanted. You'll also see how I eventually employed all the tools to Jumpstart Your Life that I'm sharing with you to get my life back on track.

In the following exercise, you'll begin to investigate the emotional power your childhood dramas hold over you. Right now, we're only concerned with deconstructing—that is, intensely examining—those dramatic and traumatic events of your past. In subsequent chapters, you'll learn to reconstruct those feelings into a more positive whole.

EXERCISE: WRITE OUT FIVE CHILDHOOD DRAMAS THAT STILL HAVE EMOTIONAL POWER OVER YOU

If you're really serious about digging into your past to see what you're hanging on to and how it affects you today, this exercise will be very revealing for you. We're about to shed some light on the family skeletons that may have been hidden away in the dark for so long that you find them overwhelming or even frightening. You may have ignored them altogether so that, looking at them now, you're no longer sure where the facts end and the fictions begin. In terms of learning to travel hopefully, it really doesn't matter what the truth is. It's your perception of the truth that is relevant. And once you expose those perceptions to the light, your childhood dramas will hold far less power over you.

Like the example I mentioned earlier of Susan who, as an adult, still believes that her disastrous tenth birthday party has contributed to her overall feelings of social awkwardness and fear of rejection, think of dramas from your childhood that may have evolved into negative life themes. Take a look at the following list to see if you can identify with any of them before you go on to list your own.

EXAMPLES OF CHILDHOOD DRAMAS

- Being ridiculed as the "fat kid" or "loser" at school or in the neighborhood
- Feeling rejection because of not getting invited to a party or social event
- Witnessing the illness of a family member or friend

- Flunking a class or bringing home a bad report card
- Being dropped by a best friend or rejected by a member of the opposite sex
- Feeling neglected by parents and other family members
- Suffering the death of a family member, friend, or beloved pet
- Not getting picked for a team
- Losing a school election
- Experiencing physical or verbal abuse by a parent or family member
- Moving away from a comfortable environment
- Living through your parents' divorce
- Coping with a physical handicap—yours or that of someone close to you
- Feeling responsible for losing a game

Here's what I want you to do:

1. Using the above list or coming up with your own examples, think of five childhood dramas that stand out in your mind today no matter how long ago they might have occurred. You can define the term "childhood" as any age that feels right to you, from toddler up to young adult. And don't think your memories have to be full-scale Dickens-worthy tragedies. They don't. Just identify any five childhood memories that still have some negative emotional power over you. By that, I mean events that were so meaningful to you then that they still affect your behavior or steer your choices today, either directly or indirectly.

2. Take a deep breath, relax, and get ready to write down your childhood dramas in your Traveling Hopefully Daybook. First, though, let's deal with any fears you might

have about writing. I'm a great believer in the power of the written word, as you'll see in this and subsequent exercises. If you haven't already, I want you to discover its magic. Although I've made my living as a writer and communications expert for some time, I had to get over all the same writing fears I'm asking you to deal with now. We're not going for perfect grammar or great art here, just honest reflection. So relax and remember that it's not the words that are important, but the feelings behind the words.

3. I want you to write a very short story—a paragraph or two—about each of the five childhood dramas you identified, giving each one a title. Give yourself a time limit of three minutes per story. Briefly summarize the circumstances as you remember them, describe your feelings around the event, and then explain why you think this memory is so important to you. If you're writing about losing a pet, was it sad and bewildering because it was your first lesson in mortality? Or was it painful because your dad didn't understand the depth of your loss and thought you were crazy to be crying over an old cat? Whatever the incident, if it left a mark on your emotional memory, it's worth exploring. So stop reading and start writing about your five childhood dramas.

MY FIVE CHILDHOOD DRAMAS

Here are the titles for my five childhood dramas. I'm only detailing one of them here as an example for you, because the others are woven throughout this book.

My Brother's Death
When I Was Molested

Meeting My Future Stepmom

Being the Poor Scholarship Kid

Dad Moves to Japan

And here is my story . . .

WHEN I WAS MOLESTED

We had a handyman who cut the grass in the yard as well as in our big pasture with a giant power mower that you ride on tractor-style. Once in a while, he'd find a den of diamondback rattlers and have to kill them, hanging the skins on the side of our old garage where he also kept his tools. When I was about eight, he asked me to come take a look at something in there. It seemed like an odd request, but he was a grown-up and I was a kid, so I did what he told me to do. When he forced me to touch him and he touched me in places I knew he shouldn't, I still didn't say anything. I wasn't raised to protest or argue. I just let him do what he had to do, then got the hell out of there. But that didn't stop it from happening again.

For a long time, I didn't tell anyone what he had done to me. I was too afraid, of what I wasn't sure. I just knew it wasn't something I wanted to tell my mother or my father or even my brothers and sisters. Finally, I told my friend Lynnie, who told her mother right in front of me. Her mother was calm and direct when she asked me question after question about the incident. My mother later asked me why I never told her, and I didn't really have an answer. I couldn't tell her that I hadn't even considered it. But I never saw that man again. That was the end of it until my father mentioned, well after my parents were divorced, that my mother had fired the handyman because she caught him flirting with our pretty young maid. I knew that wasn't why my mom had fired him, but obviously she didn't want to tell my father the truth. I always thought the whole thing was somehow my fault.

I've spent a lot of time coming to terms with my negative childhood stories so I could get past my past and get on with my life. Once we recognize who we are by understanding where we have come from, we can then begin to create a life of our own making, based on choices that will take us where we want to go. Instead of being afraid to shine the light on our negative dramas, we need to examine them, deal with them, and move past them. If we don't, we risk having an experience as devastating as molestation, or even as seemingly minor as rejection by our playmates, add more layers to an already negative family legacy.

For years, even as an adult, I felt ashamed and somehow responsible for the entire incident, as do many victims of sexual molestation. My rational mind knew that that wasn't the case at all, but emotionally I felt it was my fault. The fact that I wasn't forced, beaten, or raped, although I was certainly coerced, made it feel even more like it was my fault. I had dealt with the memory by pushing it down so deeply into my being that it was as though it had never happened.

But, as usual, the universe had it all worked out for me. I had begun collecting my thoughts for this book, never intending to discuss sexual abuse, although I know that's an issue with which far too many women can identify. A staggering one in four women has been sexually abused. Look around, if it's not you, it could be the woman at the next desk over or standing in front of you in the line at the bank who was molested. One day, I was watching an episode of *Dr. Phil* on child sexual abuse. And there was a victim, a man in this case, with virtually the same story. The molester, who was a male not only known but trusted by the family, easily lured this little boy into his trap right under his parents' noses.

I felt as though I were watching one of my darkest and most private stories unfold. When my lovely assistant Michaela, startled, asked me why I was watching this particular episode and crying my eyes out, I knew I needed to address the issue from a personal standpoint. I started to give it some serious thought. What was it that held so much power over me all these years? It was more than the shame associated with the act or the notion I'd "willingly" succumbed, but I didn't quite get it. Yet.

Just a couple of weeks later, I was summoned to jury duty. Initially, I had the same reaction most people have. Yes, it's my civic duty, but it sure is going to take a big chunk out of my life. I'd already postponed it as many times as the law would allow, so off I went to serve my time, never thinking I'd actually get picked for a case. After all, I never had before. Of course, this time I did, and guess what kind of case it was? You got it, a child sexual abuse case in which a man molested not one but three little girls, all about the same age I was when I was molested.

As I sat through everyone's testimony in this case—the girls, the medical experts, the law enforcement officers—I realized the seriousness of this crime and how similar it was to my own experience as a child. Rather than going virtually unnoticed as my case had, this guy was convicted of seventeen counts of child molestation. None of these three little girls had been beaten or drugged into submission, and yet this was a serious crime. They were seduced, because he was an adult and they were kids. He had the power, and they didn't. And he was being punished for his abuse of that power.

That's when I understood what I had missed all those years

about my negative childhood drama. I had written the whole event off as unimportant, because I'd learned a pattern of having my feelings dismissed and discounted by my own family. The people who were supposed to stand up as my protectors had all but ignored this heinous crime. Granted, that's what was done more often than not back then. Nevertheless, it was a big deal, it was a huge big deal. When I finally got that lesson — not just about the seriousness of the crime perpetrated against me, but that I had also discounted my own feelings — I vowed not to let that happen again. It took a high-stakes trial to help me rewrite the negative childhood drama of being abused. The lesson I learned is that I do not want to live my life with my voice unheard or my feelings discounted by myself or anyone else. It will happen, I don't run the planet and I can't control other people's behavior. But I will not knowingly involve myself with people who consider my feelings unimportant. My feelings are important to me as yours should be to you.

I don't know where you stand on the theory that there are no accidents, but you've got to admit, it's uncanny that just at the moment I was ready to deal with an issue that I'd been ignoring for almost forty years, I was assigned to a case that mirrored my own experience. Even you skeptics out there have to agree it's a strange coincidence. I believe that the more we are on the path of our true purpose, the more powerful healing lessons are laid in our lap. All I had to do was show up in awareness and absorb the lesson.

Not all my dramas get resolved like that, of course, as I'm sure yours won't. You've already taken a significant step forward just by identifying some of your negative stories. Depending on how you've interpreted these stories over time, they can be wonderful learning experiences that cause you to grow despite the challenges they represented at the time. Or they can be debilitating life lessons that you've allowed to sap your courage and motivation, stunting your growth and holding you back from the life you want. As you continue to experiment with the concepts in this book, envisioning the life you want and determining the best way to get it, you'll see how you can alter your perspective to rewrite these stories with more powerful and positive endings.

Now that we've begun the process of examining some of those negative personal dramas, we're going to shift gears and begin looking at the more positive moments of childhood. We'll continue to travel hopefully forward by looking back at some of our more joyful past memories. With Hopeful Tool #4, we'll explore your dreams of childhood to see what lessons those dreams might hold for you today.

Tool # 4: Recapturing the Magic of Childhood Dreams

What were your dreams of childhood? Do you remember how passionately you wanted to be a baseball player, or a dancer, or an astronaut? What was it you loved as a kid? Can you remember what it was like to touch, to taste, to feel that dream with every fiber of your being? Before adult notions like practicality, or financial reality, or other people's prejudices entered into your consciousness? Just the pure joy of being in your dream. Wouldn't you like to recapture some of that magic?

Tool #4 looks at the concept of childhood dreams and examines specific ways you can incorporate some of that magic into your life right now. Whether it's playing sports or pursuing a hobby, we're going to look at some ways you can increase your levels of relaxation and recreation. Maybe you're instinctively balking at the idea of acting like a child again, but if you're really honest with yourself, wouldn't you like a lot more play and a little less work in your life?

Whether your dream has to do with having fun or fulfilling a mission, we'll look at the value behind the dream to see what the personal significance of that dream was for you when you were a kid and what its implications are for you today. One of my dearest childhood friends remembers bandaging her brother's badly cut arm when she was nine and he was seven. Though a lot of kids would have been grossed out at the sight of all that blood, she felt the thrill of her own competence as she cleaned the gunk from the gash and stopped the bleeding. She recalls quite clearly that at that moment she knew she wanted to be a doctor.

I took dance lessons as a kid, studying ballet from elementary school all the way up through college. I remember putting on my beautiful costumes, the pink tights and ballet shoes with the ribbons laced up over my ankles, then putting on makeup, which made me feel so grown-up, and going out onstage in front of all those people with the lights shining down and the music playing. My pulse would race, I was sure I'd forget the choreography or maybe even pass out right there on the stage. There was something so exciting in the movement and the music. Although I didn't know what to call it back then, the moms said it was stage fright, it was something more for me. I was pushing myself right to the edge of my comfort zone, then going beyond it, knowing that despite the fear, I could still perform.

I was so enraptured by the entire experience of performing ballet that, for a very long time, I thought I wanted to be a professional dancer. But it wasn't my early career ambition that proved to be lasting or even significant for me. It was the value behind that dream. I had found a way to conquer my fears when I was a child, which gave me that rush of satisfaction, a taste of victory. But I lost it along the way to adulthood and longed to have that sort of passion and sense of

accomplishment back in my life, in my work, in my relationships, and in my play. Have you ever felt that you settled for
less than you really wanted somewhere along the way? That
either fear or just the circumstances of daily life caused you to
abandon the magic and power of your deepest childhood de-
sires? If I told you that you could recapture some of that passion and build it back into your life, wouldn't you want to do it?

I'm not saying you'll be a movie star or an artist at age forty-
three, although I wouldn't necessarily rule that out either.
There are countless examples of people who become doctors,
or writers, or parents even when they're initially convinced
that they're too old, too poor, or too busy to go after their
dreams. The only difference is that they have such a burning
desire, a passion to make things happen, that they do it. You're
going to end up the same age whether you go after your dream
or not, so if you want something enough, you might as well do
it. Tool #4 is the first step is to identify your dream, and, more
important, to identify the value behind the dream.

THE VALUE BEHIND THE DREAM

Here's an example of what I mean by the value behind the
dream. I recently had a consultation with a prospective coaching client named Maureen. Maureen told me she needed help
manifesting her dream to become the assistant to a certain film
actor known for his work in charitable and political causes.
Although I applauded Maureen for being able to articulate
her dream so succinctly, I cautioned her that she was limiting
her options by setting her sights on a specific job working for
a specific celebrity. What if there were no such job? Or that
job was filled already?

I urged Maureen to consider not just the dream, but the
value behind the dream. Beyond this particular job scenario,

what was it she wanted to accomplish in her work? What kind of day-to-day environment was important to her? What was it about working for a celebrity that was meaningful? As we examined her career goal more closely, Maureen's values became quite clear. She wanted to work for a person or organization that actively sought to influence people and impact our environment in positive ways.

Although someone else might have articulated exactly the same goal—to work for a celebrity—they could have had entirely different values behind the dream. They might have been looking for creative inspiration by surrounding themselves with artists, they might have been looking for the status, high pay, and first-class perks that come with working with a celebrity, or even to find a mentor in the competitive world of entertainment.

Maureen realized that, for her, the value behind the dream was the feeling of satisfaction she got from knowing she was making a difference in the world. By working for a person or organization that had an established platform and was already having positive results, she felt she could contribute the most. When she finally understood the value behind the dream, Maureen's spectrum of possibilities widened considerably and she began to brainstorm about opportunities working with nonprofit organizations and government agencies.

Looking at the value behind the dream doesn't just apply to your professional dreams, it also applies to personal ones. Maybe you're a pianist and, although you know you know it's unlikely that you'll ever play Carnegie Hall, you'd love to more actively incorporate your passion for music into your life. Where do you start?

Just like Maureen's dream of working for a celebrity, look at the values behind your dream of being a musician. Maybe what's appealing is the recognition of a crowd, the chance to be up onstage in front of an audience. Or maybe it's not about having an audience at all, but the opportunity to spend time with other musicians, entertaining yourselves and playing what you love. If you identify the value behind the dream, you'll be able to zero in on the action steps that will honor that value. If it's recognition, maybe your neighborhood symphonic group needs a pianist. If it's the joy of expression or shared love of music, maybe you can teach a high school music class or join a weekly jam session.

Sadly, many of us abandon the dream altogether because we are unable to isolate the value behind the dream and take the necessary action steps to incorporate that value into our lives. Once you start reintroducing some of the values behind those childhood dreams into your adult life, you'll be amazed at how much lighter and more joyful your world will become. And not only that, for all you overachievers out there, you'll become more focused and more productive, too.

Let's take a look some of your fondest childhood memories to see what dreams they inspired in you. Then we'll examine the values behind the dreams to see if we can recapture some of that passion today.

EXERCISE: CHILDHOOD MEMORIES AND DREAMS

---

1. Think of an occasion in your past that clearly epitomizes a wonderful childhood moment. It could be the day you hit your first home run, won the spelling bee, baked a cake with your mom, or went fishing with your dad. It doesn't have to big or dramatic, just meaningful to you. Merely thinking of it should stir up some really positive feelings; maybe a flutter is starting in your chest right now or a smile is creeping onto your face at the thought.

2. Find a comfortable place to relax, close your eyes, and let that memory play out in your mind just like a movie. Watch it from beginning to end, the event itself, how you felt about it, other people's reactions. Maybe your dream will appear in slow motion as you let those magical moments unfold before you on that giant movie screen in your mind. Take your time, have some fun with the process, and remember it's about Traveling Hopefully, not just getting there.

3. When you've got that memory pleasantly secured in your consciousness, see if you can connect that memory with a childhood dream. For example, if hitting a home run was a great moment in your young life, did it inspire you to want to be a professional baseball player or a high school coach? Did your memory of baking a cake with your mom make you want to have a big family? Or did it make you long to be a chef?

4. Now, let's look for the value behind the dream. If hitting the home run that warm summer day in Little League made you want to become a pro player, what was the value? Was it the recognition or sense that you had found something in which you could excel? Maybe that home run made you dream of becoming a coach. What was the value in your desire to coach others? Was it the feeling that you could inspire and motivate? That you were a good leader or teacher?

Dissecting a moment that inspired a childhood dream can be very revealing once you understand the value behind it. Then, and only then, can you begin to recreate those feelings in your life today. Keep a watchful eye for your own judgments about what's "good" and "bad" when it comes to values. Many of us have conflicted feelings about our own desire for money, power, or recognition. Just think of all the good you can do if you recognize those values and put them to positive use. You do yourself, and possibly others, a disservice if you ignore your own needs.

If I examine my love of dancing, which I still have today, it's partly due to the sheer joy of moving my body to music, but it's also due to the feeling of putting myself up in front of a crowd and expressing myself in some way. What is behind it is the desire to express and communicate, and if I'm being honest—as I encourage you to be—it's also the adrenaline rush of performing in front of an audience, forced to overcome my own fear. The values I attach to my positive childhood memory of dancing onstage, as well as my dream of becoming a ballerina, are the joy of expression and the desire for recognition. The question is how do I incorporate those values into my life today? I do so in my profession almost daily, as a speaker, a teacher, and a writer. Although I wouldn't attempt to be a professional dancer, I address some of those same values, though not all, through my work. The next question is, which of those values am I not incorporating and how might I build them into my life right now?

EXERCISE: SEVEN ACTIVITIES TO RECAPTURE THE VALUES BEHIND THE DREAMS

You might wonder how you incorporate the values inherent in your childhood dreams into your present-day life. Clearly, you're not performing in ballet recitals or playing Little League any more, but remember, it's not the activity, or even the dream itself, it's the value behind the dream. Let me show you a way to recapture those values. I want you to try an exercise that is very effective for getting you to shake up your thinking.

Think of seven tangible activities you can take to recapture each of the values you've identified. I ask you to name seven, knowing that you need to get your thoughts flowing and also because some will be very effective, some marginally effective, and some won't work at all.

If your childhood dream was to become a professional baseball player and you've identified the value behind the dream as the joy of physical exercise, particularly in a team setting where you have the fun and camaraderie of being with a group of pals, what would you include in your list of seven activities? I do not claim to be an athlete, but your list might look something like this:

1. Join a gym
2. Find a pickup basketball game
3. Take tennis lessons
4. Go to an adult baseball clinic
5. Coach Little League
6. Take my daughter to the batting cages
7. Join my company's softball team

Granted, you may not do all these things, but even if you do only one and bring the fun and friendship of playing sports back into your life, wouldn't that add a wonderful layer of physical exertion and good-spirited competition that may have been missing from your life?

Now commit to practicing three to five of the seven activities into your life to see what works for you. We'll talk later about timetables with measurable steps for accountability, but for now let's just identify the activities. Whether you want to recapture the thrill of pushing your limits through marathon biking, creative expression through writing, or overcoming a long-held fear through public speaking, once you begin to regularly engage in the activities that contain the values you hold most dear, you'll find you can immediately bring more excitement and energy to your life. For me, it's back to salsa class!

SUMMARY: EBB AND FLOW

Growing up alongside the banks of the St. Johns, I discovered that the river had a life of its own. Paradoxically, it was as eternal as it was ever-changing, and I learned at a young age to respect its power. When I followed its flow, it was easy for me to harness that power and navigate its waters. When I fought its current, my efforts were as futile as attempting to reverse the sunrise with the sunset. Our childhood stories have a life of their own, too. Though we can't turn the tide of those events—what happened, happened—we can control how we interpret those stories and how they affect us now.

In chapter two, we've explored the negative and positive stories of our childhood. By examining the power we've allowed our negative dramas to hold over us, we've seen how we've held ourselves back and limited our possibilities. By exploring the positive moments of our past, we've identified how the values behind those dream moments can be incorporated into our lives today. Learning to respect the currents of our lives can help us redirect the negative and build upon the positive, to flow more easily through life.

In chapter three, you'll begin to explore the concept of internal clarity by learning to turn up the volume on your inner voice through creating a healing sanctuary and meeting your future self.

3

The Cobbler's Children

The Journey to Internal Clarity

"A wounded deer leaps highest."
—Emily Dickinson

My stepmother, Fran, was one of the most bewildering, complex, lovely, pitiful women I've ever known. She was tall and thin and wore pretty clothes and bright coral-colored Chanel lipstick, very unlike my own mother, who, though always neat and tailored, never seemed to have much flair. Fran had just the tiniest hint of a Southern accent, which she hated, but I thought utterly charming. She seemed so interested in the things I loved, like books and movies and poetry, that on her good days we could talk about them for hours. But from the beginning it was clear that Fran didn't have many good days.

My stepmother, like everyone else in my family, including my parents, had a sad childhood tale. She grew up with an abusive mother and later a violent first husband, whom she'd divorced before she met my father. I thought maybe the memories of those unpleasant early days might have been the reason she spent most of our visits locked in her bedroom crying. Dad generally covered for her, saying she had a headache or was coming down with the flu or something. We knew she'd been his psychiatric patient and he'd stopped treating her when they fell in love. As I was growing up, I often wondered if he'd cured her first. Sadly, I would get my answer one day.

We first met Fran one sunny afternoon when I was about twelve, a little while before Mom and Dad were divorced. My parents had been separated for a couple of years as they waged their war over custody and money. It seemed reasonable that he had a new woman in his life. Dad had already taken all of us on a tour of the apartment Mom had been secretly sharing with her boyfriend, filled with familiar contents like her bathrobe hanging on the bedroom door and the little television set that had mysteriously disappeared from our kitchen. Both parents seemed intent on proving that the other was the adulterer, but neither, apparently, thought about what impression their accusations might leave on our young minds.

Dad picked up the five of us one muggy afternoon and took us to lunch at a pretty restaurant in old St. Augustine that was built on a pier out over the ocean. We loved to go there, because we could feed our leftovers to the huge schools of fish gathered in the water below. I remember how elegant Fran looked in her crisp summer dress and big tortoiseshell sunglasses. Not quite movie star pretty, but darn close. I thought she might have been intimidated by having so many kids thrown at her all at once, especially on top of the two she already had, but she just smiled and asked lots of questions about our favorite subjects and what we liked to do for fun.

Weeks later, my mother looked up from her newspaper one morning and asked if I'd known that my father had gotten married. I tried to keep the poker face I'd been unconsciously developing during the siege of my parents' separation. I sensed that if I admitted I was learning about my father's marriage from a column in the *Times-Union*, I'd be handing my mother a major victory. It didn't seem right to sell out my dad for being happy. I didn't know then that I would one day be forced to choose sides in a courtroom; back then I was still able to shrug off her questions. Later, I had a chance to review my own re-action to Dad's seemingly sudden nuptials, rather than my mother's. I concluded that it wasn't that my father felt the oc-casion of his second marriage wasn't important enough to tell us about. Rather, it was that we, his children, weren't impor-tant enough to tell.

Since Dad was a psychiatrist, people we knew were for-ever spinning the old joke "the cobbler's children have no shoes" to fit the shrink's kids, who, presumably, had no san-ity. Though it was always said in jest, there was an element of truth about the short supply of normalcy in our family, although it was more attributable to the parents than the offspring. We were strange, what with private investigators, phone taps, and bribery allegations all standard operating procedure in the parental repertoire.

You'd think a professional healer would have been a little more clued in to what all the post-marital mayhem might be doing to his family, but Dad didn't seem to notice. His deci-sion to include the media but exclude his own children in the news about his marriage—the day after his divorce was fi-nal—was further confirmation that my feelings, and those of my siblings, were irrelevant.

As a child it never occurred to me that my feelings should have been honored and valued, or at the very least considered, by my parents. They both seemed so consumed with living their day-to-day lives and finding ways to make each other miserable that I just got lost in the shuffle somewhere along the way. Only as an adult did I realize that being systematically diminished in this way had a profoundly negative impact on my life and that I had a lot of work to do to find the confidence I so deeply desired.

Little surprise that later on, when I was living full-time with my father and stepmother, they opted out of participating in practically every significant event of my adolescence. I pretended their absence was fine with me and that I understood that their standards were so high they might be offended by a dorky school function. I even encouraged them not to attend occasions like my high school and college graduations as well as dozens of plays and musicals in which I performed throughout school and after. Better that than ask them to come and have them decline, which was secretly my fear. The truth was, it wasn't fine. Without even realizing it, I began to build the walls of my inner fortress, brick by brick, to keep the pain at bay.

That unconscious decision to shut out as much pain, sadness, and loneliness as I could became my first line of defense in dealing with the world. I began to hide my thoughts and feelings from myself as well as others as a way to avoid the loaded questions and the general hostility that seemed to swirl around my father's and my mother's homes. My fortress walls allowed me to function, to shoulder my burdens competently enough to get me through the day. What I didn't understand, and probably couldn't have at that early stage of life, was that along with the painful feelings I was filtering out, I also shut out most of the positive feelings.

The fact that I was hitting puberty at precisely the time my parents' divorce war had escalated to its height added hormonal agitation to ongoing angst. I had no caring adult, no role model to whom I could turn to express my negative emotions that were building like steam in a pressure cooker. Lacking any sense of trust in adults or authority figures, I was far too fearful to reach out to a loving teacher, pastor, or friend's parent for solace. Instead, I turned inward as the only safe haven I could find.

CLARITY AND ACTION

That inner journey was, for me, the beginning of what I now refer to as internal clarity and external action, the second step to Jumpstart Your Life and a major component of traveling hopefully. In chapters one and two, you explored the First Step to Jumpstart Your Life, as you began to dissect your past and gain an understanding of how your family story has affected you. You also opened up some of your unwanted baggage to see how you might have turned the negative family stories into roadblocks that keep you from living the life you desire, your successes to date notwithstanding. Try the following quiz to see where you fall on the internal clarity versus external action continuum, and then we'll explore those concepts in greater depth.

QUIZ: ARE YOU AN INTERNAL DREAMER OR AN EXTERNAL DOER?

Are you a dreamer or a doer? Or have you learned to balance big-picture internal clarity with real-world external action? Try the following quiz to see where you are on the internal clarity/external action scale. Like everything you've done so far, there are no right or wrong answers, only what is truthful for you.

Rate yourself on a 1–10 scale, 1 being strongly agree and 10 being strongly disagree:

1. When you run into a problem at work or home, would you rather think it through than take action to solve it?
2. If you're contemplating a big change in your life, do you consult others for advice before making a move?
3. Is it unnecessary for people to warn you to look before you leap?
4. If you find yourself in personal or professional situations that make you miserable, do you usually understand how you got there?
5. Do you ever feel that you are being directed by some form of inner guidance or unseen wisdom?
6. Would you rather rely on gut instinct than market research?
7. Does the idea of a silent retreat—during which you don't talk, watch television, or listen to the radio for several days—appeal to you?
8. Do you generally trust your own judgment more than other people's?
9. Do you avoid acting impulsively or making snap decisions?
10. Is no decision better than the wrong decision to you?

Now let's see where you are on the continuum of internal clarity to external action. As we design your road map, you can be mindful of where you are on the scale, so you can link up these two powerful forces accordingly.

SCORING: ARE YOU AN INTERNAL DREAMER OR AN
EXTERNAL DOER?

Add up your scores on the 1–10 scale and see how you rate as
follows:

10–33   **Internal Dreamer**
         You are in touch with your internal voice and have a
         clear sense of self-guidance. You are able to trust your
         intuition, but may not always take swift or appro-
         priate action when you encounter obstacles.

34–67   **Balanced: The Dreamer Who Does**
         You are usually able to find the fulcrum between inter-
         nal vision and external action. You are generally intu-
         itive and self-aware, often taking your own, as well as
         others', viewpoints into account before acting. Once
         you've given thoughtful consideration to a problem or
         obstacle, you do not hesitate to act.

68–100   **Action Doer**
         You are the person everyone is referring to when they
         say "If you want something done, ask a busy person."
         You tend to stay in constant motion, sometimes to the
         point of collapse. But you are often disappointed that
         you don't always reap the rewards you expect, because
         you have ignored the vital internal homework to deter-
         mine a specific outcome and, instead, are merely taking
         action because you dread standing still.

As you work your way through the following Hopeful
Tools #5 and #6, you'll discover how envisioning your healing
sanctuary and meeting your future self can help you look at
your life in rewarding new ways. In this process, you'll see

how each tool builds one layer upon the next. Or perhaps, more aptly, how each tool strips away one layer and reveals the one below. While you read this chapter, be sure to keep those lessons about your negative family baggage firmly in mind. If you noted your reactions to the exercises in the first two chapters in your Traveling Hopefully Daybook, look at those again before you move forward.

Internal clarity and external action are the keys to creating the life of your dreams. First, you have to hear your inner voice and recognize the wisdom of its messages. And secondly, you have to turn those messages into action in the physical world. As we explore these concepts, you will understand what the components clarity and action mean individually, and learn how they can be inextricably linked to make your abstract big-picture vision a bottom-line reality. This understanding came in to focus gradually for me, as I drifted between households, and later countries, longing for a safe haven, a home.

After my parents divorced, Dad and Fran bought a pretty home in a small oceanside town just outside of Jacksonville, a little less than an hour from our house in Mandarin. Dad's plan was that he and Fran would settle there with her daughter, who was a year older than I, and teenage son, who would soon graduate from high school. They'd be close enough for us to visit them on weekends and far enough not to run into my mother at the supermarket.

Who harassed whom I suppose I will never know, but soon Dad claimed he could no longer live in the same state as my mother. After about a year, he was commissioned as an officer in the Navy and moved with Fran and her daughter to Washington state. It was about as far away as he could go and still be in the same country. Little did I know that soon, even that wouldn't be far enough. By giving up his private practice and joining the military, Dad was able to reduce his salary drastically, and consequently the support payments owed my mother. Dad didn't stop to consider what the overnight plunge in income would do to us. Mom put our beautiful Mandarin home on the market and we moved into an apartment complex, far away from the river.

My two sisters and I shared a bedroom, while the two boys took another, and my mother the third. As usual, we knew better than to express our feelings, ask any questions, or God forbid, complain about our reduced circumstances. Granted, things could have been much worse. We had a roof over our heads and food on our table, unlike plenty of kids, even kids right there in Jacksonville. What made things so difficult wasn't the change in lifestyle, but the inability to voice confusion or uncertainty or any negative thoughts about our changed world. One of my clearest memories of that time, other than the frightening eviction notices that were tacked to the front door whenever we made too much noise, was getting up at five A.M. to study in our bedroom's little walk-in closet so that I wouldn't wake my sisters by turning on the overhead fluorescents. There wasn't much room, but the carpet was soft and new, and I'd drag my pillow and blanket, as well as my school books, and settle down for a couple of hours all to myself. Although far from ideal, it was my first real sanctuary, a place for me to shut out the world so I could hear my own thoughts.

Tool # 5: Envisioning Your Healing Sanctuary

Learning to hear your inner voice is the first step to gaining internal clarity. While you may balk at the idea that you can actually tap into a voice in your head, even if it's your own, think about it. Chances are, you've experienced the feeling of that little voice that tells you to take the right turn instead of the left, to choose one job over another, or to go on the blind date even when you don't feel like it. Sometimes, instinctively, you just know it's the right thing to do. That's your inner voice at work.

There are a number of different ways to turn up the volume on your inner voice. To jumpstart the process, you need to create a safe and quiet space for yourself, in the physical world and in your mind. We all need a sacred place where we can re-energize, refocus, and relax. In the simple visualization exercise that follows, you will create your own vision of a healing sanctuary where you can turn down the noise of your everyday life and tune in to the richness of your inner wisdom. Do not, I repeat do not, let the term "visualization" scare you. All you need to do is read through the next section a couple of times, then set the book aside and let your mind go. Don't worry that you'll forget part of the exercise; just relax and your subconscious will do the rest. Even if you leave out a few of the steps, the important thing is that you create a mental image of your own personal healing sanctuary.

1. Once you've read through these steps a couple of times, find a comfortable spot, close your eyes and relax. Know that this will be a deeply pleasurable experience and that your mind will transport you to a sanctuary designed especially for you. There you will experience whatever you need: serenity, passion, comfort, energy, joy, or radiant health.

2. Take a few deep breaths and let any tension drain out of you. Now picture yourself, almost as if you're looking down at your own body, stretched out and in a deep state of blissfulness. Feel the warm and comforting surface upon which you're lying. Maybe it's the sand, heated by the sun, maybe it's a big fuzzy carpet, or a soft bed of pine needles. Whatever comes to you, let it form a picture in your mind. There's

no need to reach for this mental image, just let it drift to you. If it doesn't happen right away, don't worry. It will come.

3. Now take a deep breath and be aware of the scents around you. Are you inhaling the fresh breeze off the ocean? Or the pleasant aroma of food cooking in the next room? Or maybe you smell clean laundry drying outside on a clothesline. Let those scents take you back to pleasant times and places. Now listen. What do you hear? Is it the happy sounds of children playing? Or the branches of a tall tree swishing in the wind? Maybe you hear gentle waves lapping against the shore. Take a moment to breathe in the smells and hear the sounds of your environment.

4. Still lying down with your eyes closed, picture yourself reaching out from your reclining position and feeling whatever your hand comes in contact with first. Touch it, feel the surface and the texture. Is it smooth, rough, sandy? And does it link to any smells you are sensing? The lemon-scented polish on a hardwood floor or the flowers in your mental garden?

5. Now in your vision, see yourself opening your eyes and looking around. Breathe a sigh of relief as you take it all in. This is exactly, precisely the most perfect sanctuary you could have ever imagined for yourself. Whether it is a mountain cabin, a cottage on the beach, a boat out at sea, or a jungle hut, rest in the knowledge that your mind has created the perfect healing sanctuary just for you.

6. Now see yourself get up—maybe you need a luxurious stretch or maybe you bolt upright to greet your surroundings—and walk around your space. Experience your

sanctuary and sense how joyful and alive it makes you feel. Etch this feeling on your mind, because you'll be coming back here often. Take a moment and capture your sanctuary as a painting, a photograph, or a movie in your mind. Again, don't reach for the vision. Trust that it will come.

7. Next, you spot a beautiful treasure that holds the gift of a special word for you. This treasure is something from your sanctuary, maybe it's a lovely seashell or an intricately carved wooden box. Pick it up and hold it in your hand. Feel its texture, inhale its fragrance. Then open it up or turn it over to uncover your gift, which is a word written on your treasure—however you see it—just for you. Let the word come to you and know that this word holds deep meaning for your life. Maybe the word you see in your treasure is peace, love, harmony, or strength. Remember this word and add it to your vision, so that you can revisit this place anytime you need the power of your word. This is your healing sanctuary and the word is a treasure from your inner wisdom, the beginning of inner clarity. Use it well. When you are ready, open your eyes and bring your focus back to the real world.

MY HEALING SANCTUARY

From the time I was a kid studying in the walk-in closet, I began to regularly call up my vision of a healing sanctuary. I needed the strength and consolation it gave me to know that if I could envision a beautiful place of great peace and joy, that someday I would find that place. The details of my sanctuary are not as important as the details of your own, but I will share them with you in a minute so that, together, we can reinforce the idea of healing through internal clarity, the clarity you find by tuning in to your inner voice. Creating your healing sanctuary gives you the solidity of a home base in which you can find the silence you need to tune out the negative baggage of your family legacy and the overwhelming demands of your daily life. Unlocking the peaceful power of your healing sanctuary will also help you learn to call upon the positive feelings you want at your disposal, when you want them, not when the outside world deigns to bestow them upon you. Your peace and your joy are in your control.

I don't know when I first visualized my healing sanctuary or when I knew that that's what it was. For many years, I have seen a clear vision in my mind of a lovely little house on the cliffs up above the ocean. It's very quiet and still; all I can hear are the sounds of the waves below and the breeze ruffling the white curtains of my living room. The floors of my home are made of a beautiful glossy wood, with only one soft white rug covering the center area. The furniture is all cream-colored, overstuffed and luxurious. The windows reach from floor to ceiling, with the most incredible ocean view imaginable. The curtains are made of a gauzy white fabric that billows in the soft breeze. This peaceful little home is my healing sanctuary, and I have no doubt that someday it will be as tangible and real for me in the external world as it is in my clear internal vision. Meantime, I can visit it in my mind whenever I need its calming spirit.

Your sanctuary may be as grandiose as your own resort set on a private tropical island or a sophisticated luxury apartment with sweeping skyline views. It might be as simple as a cabin in the woods or a hammock in the backyard. Or you may have several healing sanctuaries that serve different needs from peacefulness to excitement.

Even if this exercise feels somewhat abstract or maybe even silly to you, disciplining yourself enough to still your mind and let the images wash through your brain can be a very restorative act. As you quiet the constant critical play-by-play that you're used to running in your head and simultaneously tune out the noise of your daily life, you'll be amazed at the sense of serenity and clarity that will develop over time. Eventually, you'll hear a new voice, that of your own inner guide, become louder, clearer and more intense as it steers you through the decisions, big and small, of your daily life.

MY FUTURE SELF

Growing up, I'd been one of the few in my family who actively sought religion. My parents were Unitarians, but since there was only one Unitarian church in Jacksonville and it was on the other side of the county, they rarely made the effort. My father made God jokes and claimed to be an agnostic, being too much of a scientist, he said, to accept things on faith. My mother just seemed indifferent or stumped by it all, or maybe God had deeply disappointed her already.

When I was in elementary school, I began my weekly pilgrimages to the All Saints Episcopal Church on Mandarin Road, about a quarter of a mile walk from our house. Often I went alone; sometimes, if they felt inspired, my mother or one of the other kids would join me. The church itself was beautiful, an old wooden edifice with a big stained glass window facing the waterfront. When it was destroyed in a hurricane, they rebuilt a new church overlooking the river. That church was beautiful and much bigger, but I missed the little wooden one.

We were a small community so, of course, we knew the minister and his entire family. Maybe that's why it never felt strange for me to go to church and Sunday school all by myself. Maybe it was because I loved putting on my robes and my chapel cap in the anteroom, then singing hymns in the choir with the other neighborhood kids. Partly it was the magic of the ceremony in that sacred spot, but mostly it was because I sensed God was out there somewhere, and if I could just find him he could help me deal with my pain and loneliness. That lovely little church provided an early sanctuary for my inner searching.

Even as a regular church-goer, I was not really one of the congregation. We were Unitarians, after all, and we did not believe that Jesus Christ was the son of God, but I wasn't really an Episcopalian either because I didn't get confirmed or take communion like the other kids. I stopped going to church after we moved from Mandarin, but I continued to listen for that voice of God, which I now know comes in many forms, including our own internal clarity.

My relentless search for self, though I didn't know to call it that back then, would soon take me halfway around the world. My father, claiming that my mother was harassing him mercilessly every time he came to visit us in Florida, accepted a commission at a Navy hospital in Yokosuka, Japan. While Dad went on to live what seemed to be an exotic and dashing adventure with his new wife and substitute daughter, my mother struggled to make ends meet and maintain some sort of dignity. We were no longer the doctor's family with the beautiful country home. We had become middle-class kids with a distant dad, a working mom, and a new stepfather who drank too much.

At age fourteen, I was developing an inner sense of the kind of person I wanted to become. Some burning desire within pushed me to move past my pain and keep trudging forward. I began to form an image of a woman who could serve as a kind of guide or role model—someone whom I wanted in my life to show me what I could become in the future. How could I have that person nearby to guide and comfort me? And how could I learn to grow into a caring and compassionate adult?

Around the time I was turning into a teenager, I began to
sense the image of an older woman who I often felt was watching over me. That woman wasn't a ghost or a dearly departed
ancestor. She was a mental vision of someone who was close
by and could answer my questions or make me feel better
when I was sad. I always wished this woman would sit down at
the kitchen table with me and help me solve my dilemmas and
the problems of the world, but I had no such person in my life,
only in my imagination.

Eventually, when I felt especially lost, I would conjure
up her face, her body, even her clothing and see her quite
clearly. I would tell her what was bothering me, and
she would help me sort things out. She was direct and honest, occasionally even blunt, but never less than loving. I
wanted this woman, or at least her image, to be accessible
to me all the time. If we couldn't really sit together at the
kitchen table discussing every aspect of life, then we'd discuss those things in my vision. She was a grown-up version
of an imaginary playmate. I knew she wasn't real, but I
could count on her wisdom and strength to see me through
my difficulties.

The more adept I became at communicating with my imaginary mentor, the more I began to realize that this vision was
me—my future self. I was calling upon my own innate wisdom
and compassion for self-guidance. I really liked this person,
this older, wiser woman whom I would become. I did not wish
to leave this relationship to chance—either the ongoing communication with her or the long-term metamorphosis into becoming her. Instead, I began to look for ways to build that
connection to self into my life.

Maybe you already have a sense of the kind of person you
want to grow into. Or maybe you're afraid that you stopped
growing a long time ago, and that's why you were drawn to

this book. Meeting your future self can help you define who you are today and who you want to become in the future.

Tool # 6: Meeting Your Future Self

The following exercise is designed to help you tap in to your internal clarity as you did in envisioning your healing sanctuary. The first part of the exercise will be written, the second part is a visual meditation. I encourage you to write out your reactions in your Traveling Hopefully Daybook, so you can begin to identify recurring themes about the person you want to become and the life you want to live. We'll begin to implement actions based on your internal vision a little later.

IDENTIFYING FIVE CHERISHED CHARACTERISTICS OF YOUR FUTURE SELF

We've all asked or been asked "What do you want to be when you grow up?" I'm asking you to reframe that question with the emphasis on the personal rather than the professional — "Who do you want to be when you grow up?" Regardless of your current age, what personality traits do you want to develop or strengthen in yourself? Would you like to be more compassionate or fun-loving? Would you like to be more adventurous or risk-taking? And what characteristics do you want to minimize or redirect? Maybe you'd like to be less anxious or distrustful, or to learn to manage your stress.

I want you to think of yourself as objectively as possible. What are the five most important characteristics you must possess to be the best person you can be? I'm not saying you'll develop all these traits overnight, that's why we're looking ahead at your future self. If you were to sit down at the kitchen table right now and share a meal with the future you, who would you want that person to be? What qualities would that person have to possess to be so special to you?

Take a look at the following list of cherished characteristics to see if some of them belong on your list. In a moment, I'm going to ask you to list the five traits which are most important in your future self. If you already possess some or all of those characteristics, great; you're on your way to becoming your future self. And, if not, you can begin now by identifying what those traits are.

Your list might include some of these characteristics:

Confident

Curious

Powerful

Serene

Determined

Motivated

Ambitious

Focused

Fun-loving

Adventurous

Passionate

Open-minded

Kind

Accepting

Now, here's what I want you to do next:

Make a list of the five cherished characteristics that your future self must possess. Sometimes one word doesn't have enough nuance to express what you're trying to say, so feel free to expand or clarify those characteristics. As you'll see from my list, I qualified my adjectives so they felt more specific and customized to the person I want to be.

My list looks like this:

FIVE CHERISHED CHARACTERISTICS OF MY FUTURE SELF

Compassionate—kind and caring toward myself and others

Joyful—lighthearted, low-stress sense of fun and adventure

Spiritual—connected to my inner self, the physical world, and the unseen universe

Communicative—expressive and creative

Energetic—full of life, risk-taking

MEETING YOUR FUTURE SELF

Next, we're going to create a visual image of your ideal future self, the self who will embody all those characteristics you just identified. If you have a mental picture of that future self, it will be much easier for you to call upon that inner vision when you need guidance. Not only will this image provide you with a way to tap into your own internal wisdom, it will point the way toward the self you want to develop. This is where internal clarity begins to link with external action. Don't worry if the concept is not yet crystal clear for you. It will be as we move forward.

1. First, find a comfortable spot to sit or lie down and relax fully. Now that you've had some experience with relaxation and visualization exercises, you've probably found a place in your home or office that is a comfortable spot for

you. Establishing a special "relaxation spot" can help pre-condition your mind to be open and peaceful even before you start. Lie down, breathe deeply, and let all your tension and stress melt away.

2. Envision the peacefulness of your healing sanctuary, step onto a path just beyond it, and start walking. Note your senses as you walk — smell, sound, sight, touch. Now, look ahead in the distance, where you see a person. You can't quite make out the form or gender just yet. Even at this distance, you get a sense of power and energy. As you approach, you can begin to feel the presence of the five cherished characteristics within this person's being. Now, begin to see your future self, that is, the person into whom you would like to evolve, whether that is tomorrow or twenty years from now. Take in his or her appearance including gender, age, clothing, and manner. Do you see, feel, or hear those cherished characteristics? How are they manifesting in your future self? Is there a kind expression? A warm demeanor? A wicked laugh? What emotions do you feel coming from this person? Make sure you distinguish each of those cherished traits you identified.

3. Now see your current self greeting your future self. As you take in each other's essence, see the physical attitude and hear the conversation. Ask for the kind of guidance and support you need.

4. Now sense the two of you melding together into one being. Whether it's through an embrace or some other form of connection, see yourself becoming your future self and know that this wiser, kinder, more powerful self is there for you, not just in the future but right now. Finally, give

this future self a name (if it's your name, that's okay) so that you can call upon him or her any time you want.

Whenever I visualize my future self, I see a woman of about sixty-five or seventy, who looks incredibly youthful for her years. She's tall and thin with an athletic body and dark gray hair, pulled back into some kind of bun or braid. She's usually wearing a soft, pajamalike pantsuit in a rich navy. Her eyes are bright blue, sparkling with intelligence. And even though she could skewer me with her killer wit and irreverent sense of humor, she doesn't. She's far too kind and compassionate, and, somehow, she always knows just the right thing to say to make me feel better about my life. This is the woman with whom I'd like to sit down at my kitchen table and have a heart to heart over a good bottle of wine. And this is the woman I'd like to become.

I could not find the compassionate guidance I sought in either my mother or my stepmother. I don't blame either of them for their inability to be the kind of role model I wanted in my life; they lacked that kind of loving role model in their lives, too. Instead, I invented a rich inner world where I could find the nourishment I craved. At first, that nourishment was self-made and imaginary. Now, I've learned to translate that loving inner vision into external reality through my friendships, loving relationships, and meaningful work that feeds me emotionally. That's the unmistakable, unstoppable power of linking internal clarity with external action.

SUMMARY: BELIEVING YOUR INNER VISION

There is an old Hopi saying, "You have to believe in gods to see them." Thoughts and actions are very much like that. First you conceive your thoughts, then you act your thoughts

into being. You believe, then you see. It may seem counterintuitive, since most of us have been brought up on the notion
that seeing is believing. As you begin to believe in the vast-
ness and power of your internal clarity, you will see it manifest in external action.

As we've seen in this chapter, creating a healing sanctuary
and meeting your future self are just two ways to build the
muscle of internal clarity. In chapter four, you'll begin to link
that inner awareness to the external world by learning to recognize your recurring life themes by finding yourself in fairy
tales, myths, and literary works. You'll also take the power of
the written word to a deeper, more meaningful level by looking at life themes through verbal meditation.

4

Life in the Lonely Castle

Learning to Recognize Recurring Life Themes

"Knowing others is wisdom,
knowing yourself is enlightenment."

—Lao-tzu

I have been told that the Japanese have an ancient custom of passing prized family soup recipes from one generation to the next. This is accomplished not by handing a written recipe down the generational line, but rather by giving a pot of the soup to younger family members so that they can continue the culinary tradition. As a result, the family maintains a kind of never-ending soup base, to which each subsequent generation adds its own distinctive flavor variations. As we've seen in the last few chapters, family legacies are very much like that soup. Our ancestral stew is just the starting point. Whether we cook up a toxic family soup or improve upon the base is entirely up to us.

My mother's and father's ancestral stews shared a common ingredient; that seemingly random coincidence might have been the link that, consciously or not, drew the two of them together. My paternal grandfather was a drug-addicted, small-town country surgeon who ran a thriving illegal abortion clinic in rural Texas. My maternal grandmother, married with two children and pregnant with a third, bled to death following an illegal abortion when my mother was five years old. These disconnected occurrences, in fact years and states apart, set the tone for my parents' upbringings. My father grew up in a house of silent shame, and my mother was farmed out to a series of relatives. Their experiences set in motion their recurring themes of emotional distance and lack of trust that played out time and time again throughout my young life. Not surprisingly, my parents' themes had a direct impact in shaping my own, particularly my recurring feelings of loneliness and unworthiness that I struggled with for many years. In this chapter, we'll look at the recurring themes in our lives and how we've allowed the negative ones to limit our choices and rob us of the life we want. At the same time, we'll see how picking positive themes can provide us with great inspiration and happiness.

After my dad, stepmother, and stepsister moved to Yokosuka, I visited in the summer months. Instead of the every-other-weekend visits typical for kids of divorce, our routine was for Dad to fly to Jacksonville to pick us up, we'd head to San Francisco, then on to Japan. One summer, it was my older brother Bill and I, another it was my younger sister and brother, Ruth and Cameron, and I. I was always included. I wouldn't have missed those months in Japan with my father for anything. After a couple of summer visits, I asked to live with my dad full-time. As a young teen, I'd long since outgrown my Southern surroundings. My sister Ruth followed suit, literally as it turned out, and we both went to court to petition for a change of custody. When the judge granted my father a year's custody based on the cultural benefits of our living abroad, we didn't realize the price we would pay for choosing him over our mother. She would later refuse to let us return.

For a small-town girl from Florida, seeing the sights from San Francisco to Tokyo was a dream come true. Now a "navy brat" at fifteen, everything seemed like an exotic adventure—from our international high school in Yokohoma to our on-base housing in a former courthouse dubbed "the castle" because of its unusual castlelike rooftop.

Dad seemed to have readjusted to his former military status with ease; for our stepmother Fran it was sometimes a more challenging fit. Her retreats behind the locked doors of her bedroom, though less frequent, seemed more intense. Eventually, I learned about her failed suicide attempts and feared that someday she would succeed, though I never discussed it with anyone.

Communication with Fran was often more mystifying than the language barrier we experienced with the Japanese. On one particularly memorable trip in the dead of winter, Dad, Fran, and the three of us girls went to visit the temple city of Kyoto. Breathtakingly beautiful, Kyoto is revered by the Japanese as the sacred city of ancient temples and historic sites.

Fran, in a display of chilliness that rivaled Kyoto's bitter winter, decided to stop speaking to me throughout our stay. Apparently enraged over my choice of wardrobe for our trip, which was my customary school attire of skirts and sweaters, she refused all direct communication with me. She would address me only through my father who, inexplicably, went along with her bizarre behavior as though it were completely normal. Whether Fran was offering my dad some scathing commentary about my clothing or appearance or providing a bit of historical data about the sights we were seeing, Dad would dutifully pass her message along to me, as though I might not understand. What I didn't understand was what I had done to make Fran so angry. By this point in my life, I no longer expected anyone, especially my father, to discuss or explain these sorts of outbursts or protect my feelings.

There I was, a fifteen-year-old girl living in a castle in a foreign land, wondering if I was crazy and everyone else was normal. Or if I was normal and everyone else was crazy. I wasn't sure anymore and had no reasonable adult to whom I could turn for guidance in navigating my often bewildering existence. I retreated into books, devouring plays and historical fiction as my escape. Sometimes my dad would speak to me, and I'd look up from whatever I was reading with a blank stare, as if I had no connection to my earthly surroundings. My body was present, but the rest of me had been transported elsewhere. I thought of my family as a cautionary fairy tale, with me at its center: the father, well-meaning but oblivious; the wicked stepmother, singling out the heroine for punishment; the sisters, one older and one younger, sullen and jealous. I was the tragic heroine, the misunderstood middle daughter, who longed one day to prove herself to be kind, loving, and courageous.

I began to identify with literary figures from Jane Eyre to Cinderella, barely stopping to think about the messages I was absorbing about who I was and where I fit into the world. What were the themes that were beginning to develop, take root and recur? And how would these self-beliefs either limit or expand my life?

RECURRING LIFE THEMES

Next, we'll look at universal themes and familiar characters — in fairy tales, legends and literature — with which you identify.

We'll go deeper into recognizing your recurring themes and identifying negative patterns with a writing exercise.

There are many different methods of learning. Some of us respond well to methods like the fairy tale exercise that follows, others respond better to more linear exercises like defining goals and building an action map. That's why I've given you many different types of tools in this book. I encourage you to try them all, then return to the ones that work best for you and build them into your ongoing Traveling Hopefully journey. Even if a tool seems difficult or just plain foreign to your thinking, try it anyway. That's precisely the point: to shake up the way you think and move through the world by trying on a completely new perspective. In fact, the more resistant you are to an exercise, the more strongly I suggest you tackle it.

Remember the concept of flip-side logic and how you changed some of your negative perceptions to positive ones immediately, in the moment? Keep that in mind as you use the following tool. It is designed to help you recognize your recurring themes by looking at the stories that strike an emotional chord in you and identifying more positive outcomes.

Tool # 7: Finding Yourself in Fairy Tales, Myths, and Literary Works

What fairy tale characters, literary figures, or archetypes resonate with you? Which plots or storylines seem to hold a message that is particularly meaningful? Have you ever thought about why Superman or Snow White mean more to you than just kid stuff? Were you the little girl who always felt like an outcast? Or the boy who wanted to be so powerful that he could leap tall buildings in a single bound? Fairy tales, with their archetypal characters and universal stories of right and wrong, good and evil, happy and sad, evoke powerful feelings in people. That's why these stories have existed for centuries, all over the world.

There are many ways to learn to recognize recurring themes in your life. Are you the perpetual victim, the loner, the loser, or the chaos-creator? How about the rescuer or the playboy? Looking at your life as a literary work is just one way to see yourself more clearly. Whether it's a fairy tale, a Greek tragedy, or Roman myth, when you look at universal themes you can often find yourself somewhere in the story.

Since I first read the novel in the eighth grade, I have identified very closely with the tragic heroine Jane Eyre. Alone, unloved, underestimated, and overworked, Jane tries to provide the kind of compassion and protection for her pupil Adèle that she so desperately wants for herself. Finally, after years of loneliness and hardship, she prevails, finding love and fulfillment.

Maybe you think of yourself as a literary figure like Oliver Twist, abused and unwanted. Perhaps you're King Arthur, deceived by your true love and betrayed by your best friend. Or maybe you have your own version or variation—a personal fairy story—that resonates with you. Are you the Wounded Prince, desperately seeking comfort or salvation? Or the Angry Wife, always lashing out at the ones she wants most to protect? Or the Shining Venus, an earth mother who radiates joy and love?

Identifying a compelling character with whom you feel a deep sense of kinship can be a profound, unsettling, thrilling experience. It can be particularly meaningful if you are able to determine exactly what it is about that character that so moves you, and whether that association is life-enhancing or restricting. You may know immediately with which literary figures or fairy tale characters you identify, but if not, take a look a list below to give you some ideas, then try the following exercise.

FAIRY TALE, MYTHICAL, OR FICTIONAL CHARACTERS

Snow White

The Incredible Hulk

Venus

Superman

Oliver Twist

Jack (of Jack and the Beanstalk)

The Princess (of the Princess and the Pea)

David Copperfield

Beauty or the Beast

Aquaman

Peter Pan

Cinderella

Prince Valiant

Zeus

Rapunzel

The Wicked Witch

Mona Lisa

David (of David and Goliath)

Joseph

Hamlet

Noah (of Noah's Ark)

Here's what I want you to do:

1. Identify a literary, fairy tale, or mythical figure who has special meaning for you and your life. List five character traits of that figure.

2. See if you can establish the link between yourself and the character you've chosen. In other words, what do the two of you have in common? Is this a positive, happy association or is it painful for you to think of yourself sharing traits with this character?

3. List three key plot points to the particular story from which your character is derived. Then, look for any themes that your life story shares with the fictional story you identify with.

4. Finally, see if you can think up a new ending or more positive twist to the fairy tale, myth, or literary work with which you identify. That is, if you could wave your magic wand and change the outcome of the story, how might it end? If it's a negative story, how would you make it right? If it's a positive story, how would you make it even better?

Here's my exercise:

1. Jane Eyre is my literary figure. Her five characteristics are: undervalued, unloved, hardworking, subservient, and smart.

2. Similarities to me are very clear. I have often felt lonely and unloved. I have always worked very hard, often felt it was unappreciated or even unnoticed. I have always been

confident that I am bright, but often felt that it hasn't gotten me very far so I must be doing something wrong.

3. Plot points are: Jane goes to take care of Adèle, Jane falls in love with someone who is unavailable to her, Jane leaves heartbroken and despondent. Again, like me, she works really hard and often feels completely alone. Note that I picked out all the negative story points and ignored all the positive ones. I didn't do that for your benefit; that's just how it translated for me.

4. If I were to wave the magic wand, I would have everyone at Mr. Rochester's estate notice immediately how special, bright, and beautiful Jane is. She would radiate love throughout the household. Mr. Rochester and Adele and all the servants would adore her immediately. Mr. Rochester would be single (no insane wife in the attic upstairs), no fire, no tragedy. We'd cut to the happy ending much sooner and with far less struggle. And, of course, we would all live happily ever after.

It's not the specific plot points we're after here, but what the plot says about the character with whom you identify as well as your overall story. What sticks with you about a particular story and why? And how does the theme or self-belief you share with the character in the story affect your life? Jane Eyre's story of the poor, put-upon governess—the outsider on the fringes of a better life—who never gave up despite her struggles, has always struck a chord with me. Like Jane, I have plodded on at times without any idea what was keeping me going. I have tried to maintain my dignity and self-reliance, but lost out on a lot of happiness by adhering to my limiting life theme that I was alone and that if I reached out, no one would be there for me. It took me a long time to realize that I could change my beliefs and identify with the positive parts of Jane's character and her story. Or I could simply find other stories with themes that expanded my life and brought me inspiration instead of hanging on to dreary, depressing themes. Only now as I look back can I see how many times there actually was someone there extending a hand to me. Teachers, friends, employers. But I had refused to acknowledge those outstretched hands for fear that if I reached out, they would be withdrawn.

When I went to a college reunion a while back, a woman who was an upperclassman when I was an incoming freshman told me a story about myself that made me recognize this recurring life theme. I remembered the incident, but I was shocked at her telling of the story—and how telling it was about me. On my first day of college, scared out of my wits but determined to follow my dream to be an actress, I auditioned for a play. The play was Clare Booth Luce's *The Women*. Since the entire cast was female, I figured I had a decent shot at getting a part. I got a part, a bit one, but a part nonetheless. I was hooked. I marched right up to the registrar's office and declared myself a theater major. What I didn't know until that moment was all new theater majors had to perform three monologues in front of the entire department of students, staff, and faculty.

Completely clueless about where to begin, I went to the department's script library and told the student librarian I wanted to check out some plays. The librarian, the woman who later told me this story, was a hotshot acting major and the premiere leading lady within the department. She'd performed most of the female leads, directed plays, and sung in musicals. She was the greatest possible resource I could have had. And she offered to help me find the three monologues I would need to perform.

"No thanks," I told her, "I don't need any help." And so I checked out a stack of plays and went back to my apartment to start panicking. True to my life-limiting theme, I believed that I was meant to tackle this task completely alone. Starting with my own family, I rarely asked for help or took it when it was freely offered, and I didn't plan to start now just because I was a clueless incoming freshman. I was so green I didn't even know people expected me to be clueless. Instead, I struggled through the entire process alone and somehow pulled it off. But what should have been an exhilarating introduction into my new major, and what I hoped would one day be my career, was a frightening and lonely experience. On some deep level, I was terrified that the leading lady script librarian would discover that I was a phony. Inept, unworthy, not even deserving of my little spot in the theater department of my state college. Yet, rather than look at those erroneous themes that I used as a basis for much of my decision-making, I tried to tell myself I was very grown-up and self-sufficient. Just think how my world might have expanded had I found the courage to say "I don't know" or "I need help."

When she reminded me of this encounter years later, the former student librarian told me what "an arrogant snot" she thought I was. An arrogant snot, I thought? Me? I thought I had been so mature and diligent and hardworking. Just like Jane Eyre. Well, that's not what she experienced. She had held out her hand to me, and I had smacked it. She was my fairy godmother ready to wave the magic wand, and I had deprived her of the opportunity to help me. Maybe she was right; maybe I had been an arrogant snot.

One of my key life themes—the lonely, hardworking, self-sufficient girl—had not served me in this instance. All it had done was make me work harder and feel more alone. I may not have gotten it then, but I certainly get it now, and I've done a lot of internal homework to flip this kind of limiting self-belief in order to alter my external life circumstances. By eliminating the restrictive theme of "I am all alone" and replacing it with the belief that "there's plenty of help available to me," I've been able to improve my life dramatically.

Tool # 8: Looking at Life Themes Through Verbal Meditation

Next we'll look at verbal meditation, a potent tool in pinpointing life themes and their resultant behavioral patterns. When you record these verbal explorations in your Traveling Hopefully Daybook, you'll be amazed at how clearly and powerfully your recurring themes, and the choices you make based on those beliefs, will jump off the page, sometimes smacking you right in the face with solutions so easy and obvious that you'll wonder how you ever missed them.

When I lived in Japan in my teens, I thought it would be very sophisticated to keep what I called my travel journal. I'd jot down interesting anecdotes from our trips around the country, I'd philosophize about the cultural differences between Westerners and Asians, I'd make mention of handsome men or exotic women I saw on the train or shopping on the Ginza. What began as a sort of running travelogue soon became a written refuge for me, a place to register my most private thoughts about the controlled hysteria that always seemed to be simmering just below the surface in our castle home. Whether it was my father's drinking, Fran's depression, or my first crush on the boy in geometry, my travel journal soon became my confidante, trustworthy, private and always on my side. I began to write with great abandon. And I discovered it felt really good to pour out my troubles and ask for help in finding solutions.

Anyone who takes part in any sort of single-focused activity—like running, woodworking, or playing guitar—knows how relaxing and at the same time energizing it can be to narrow our focus. In this world of multitasking in which most of us are chronically overstimulated, doing just one thing in a focused way can feel luxurious. That's exactly what I like about writing. It's that feeling of shutting out the rest of the world while your brain switches to autopilot and just drives itself. It's liberating, and it's creative. And it's what we're going to do next.

Okay, don't start up the internal monologue on your fear of writing. Like the other written exercises we've tackled, this one has nothing to do with grammar, art, or perfection. Your aim is to get a free-flowing meditation going, to look at your recurring themes, and to learn to frame powerful questions that will prompt powerful solutions. Once you get the knack of this simple question and answer format, you can literally problem-solve in your sleep. Wouldn't it be refreshing to wake up every now and then with the answer to one of your niggling questions staring you right in the face?

Once you begin to make verbal meditation a habit, you'll be shocked at the ease with which you spot your own self-defeating patterns, get answers to specific questions from parenting problems to relationship dilemmas, and unleash your own creative juices—precisely what you need in order to help you envision the life you want and create the action plan to make it happen. You can apply the verbal meditation techniques I'm about to describe to virtually any tool in this book, recording your reactions and going deeper into your internal and external processes. For now, I'll focus on recurring life themes.

First off, I'm going to tell you a little bit about my process of verbal meditation, then later I'll show you a typical example from my Traveling Hopefully Daybook. Here's my routine for verbal meditation: I take ten to fifteen minutes, four days or so a week, and sit down with my daybook. I've made it a real point to create a space and time that is enjoyable for me because if you repeat something and it is pleasurable, it's easy to become addicted to that activity. You have to find a way to make verbal meditation habitual, like physical exercise, in order to program yourself for success. Once you begin to see the results you'll gain through the magical power of the written word, you'll be hooked.

I usually start my verbal meditation by writing about my status (date, location, top-line events of my daily life) as well as my current feeling state. Am I lonely? Sad? Overworked? That way, I have a frame of reference for what was going on in my life, both internally and externally, when I return to my verbal meditation later on. Looking back at your meditations as the pages begin to pile up can reveal themes and patterns. I begin the process of focusing my internal clarity so I can begin to take positive external action to counteract my negative life themes.

There are a couple of ways to do this. First, identify a recurring life theme as I have with my Jane Eyre story and narrow it down to one specific aspect that is particularly timely or troubling for you. In my case, I'll look at my inability to ask for help. Clearly, being able to request help as I needed it could have made my life much less burdensome and far more enjoyable. So how do I use my meditation to get at some meaningful answers about my refusal to seek help?

You can try the free-flowing meditation by stating your life theme and adding the word "because" after it, like this: "I refuse to ask for help, because . . ." Then let yourself write for ten or fifteen minutes, filling in the blanks on your topic. Don't censor yourself, just let it come. It may take a few attempts, but you'll be amazed at how quickly your subconscious will take over and begin to reveal some answers for you about your negative themes and patterns.

Or you can pose a specific question, what I call a powerful question. Questions can be tricky, because in order to get the right answers, you've got to first ask the right questions. This may take a little practice, so be patient with yourself. The key to asking the right question is to make sure you hit the issue you're grappling with head on. For example: Why am I so afraid to ask for help?

When you're posing your own powerful question, be sure to frame it in simple, straightforward language that calls for a direct, easy to understand response. If the question requires that the answer include specific action steps as part of the solution, so much the better. Another way to use powerful questions effectively is to pose the question at night right before you go to bed, by writing it out in your daybook—again in strong, direct language that calls for a specific response. Look at the question again when you wake up in the morning and sit down to write. Write out your response to the question as that day's verbal meditation.

Let's try both these scenarios on one of your recurring life themes—the free-flowing meditation and the use of powerful questions. You can try both of these tools right now, then adapt them as needed to your best time and place of the day. Don't forget to set yourself up for success by making this tool stimulating and fun.

FREE-FLOWING MEDITATION

1. Find a spot in your home where you can write for ten or fifteen minutes every day without being interrupted. It should be somewhere comfortable and comforting.

2. Take out your Traveling Hopefully Daybook, give each entry a heading (I always include date, time, place). Then state your recurring life theme as a "because" sentence and start writing. For example, "I refuse to ask for help, because . . ."

3. Keep your hand moving across the page, even if you think you're not saying much. Just keep writing for about fifteen minutes or three pages, whichever feels right to you.

POSING POWERFUL QUESTIONS

1. Before you go to bed at night, think about the recurring theme with which you've been struggling. Relax into your question and know that the universe is a kind place and can help you to find the answers you're looking for, if you frame your inquiry in a clear and direct fashion.

2. Now write your powerful question at the top of the page in your daybook. Again, make it clear, concise, and answerable. It can be a general question about your theme, such as "Why do I find it so difficult to ask for help?" Or it can be more specific to events in your life that relate to your negative patterns. For example, maybe your powerful questions are: Why didn't I ask my husband for the help I needed? Why am I afraid to ask for more help at work? Your powerful questions might include the following: Why do I need other people's validation? Why can't I find an appropriate partner? What kind of risks can I take to make my life more adventure-filled? How can I feel more passion about my work and in my marriage?

3. Your questions can involve big issues or everyday concerns; the concept is the same. Ask a clear question that has a real answer. Don't set up iffy hypotheticals or long-winded scenarios. Yes or no, this or that, what action steps to take—those are the most effective and answerable types of question.

4. The next morning, as soon as you get out of bed, take your daybook off your nightstand, open it up, and look at your question. Now go write out your verbal meditation, but this time focus on the question and let the answer come. You won't always get the answer right away, but eventually it will come. You just have to keep writing and focusing on honing your internal clarity.

After you've been at it for a while, say a couple of weeks, and have begun to develop your own style of verbal meditation, take a look back through your daily entries. See if either the free-flowing or the powerful questions method works better for you, or maybe it's a combination of the two. Are you beginning to gain any clarity about your recurring life themes? Are you able to see some actions that might address your negative behavior patterns and bring you desired changes? Make any course corrections—that is, changes to the format or content—that you think would make this a more valuable tool to have in your repertoire of exercises to link internal clarity and external action.

Now that I've explained the concept of verbal meditation as well as the two primary methods for putting that tool into practice, I'll give you some examples from my own daybook. Again, I'll start with the recurring life themes I identified through my Jane Eyre story. I've already focused on the "refusing to ask for help" aspect of that theme; now I'll look at the related theme of loneliness through both verbal vehicles, free-flowing meditation and powerful questions.

Here's my free-flowing meditation:

I am lonely because . . . I believe that I am not worthy of company. I am inherently unloveable and destined to live my life either alone or with unsuitable partners. No one of character, integrity, passion, or action could ever love me. I better find some hobbies or get a couple of cats, because I am sure to live my life alone.

No, I refuse to give in to that. I may have succumbed to the belief that I was unlovable and would, therefore, live my life alone, but I no longer believe that. I am worthy of love. I am honest, funny, smart, and curious about the world. I'm a good mom, and I have extremely satisfying, positive relationships with my sons. I have wonderful friendships with smart, strong, fun-loving adults. And I know I will find a loving partner to be my husband and spend the rest of my life with.

And here's my powerful question meditation:

How can I stop feeling so lonely?

I can stop feeling so lonely by remembering to reach out when I'm troubled. I have worked hard to build a network of loving friends and recognize that though none of them can meet all my needs, all of them can meet some of my needs. When I am feeling rejected or overstressed, I do not have to remain alone. I can call a friend who is upbeat and adventurous like Janet, and suggest we get some kind of pampering, like a massage or facial and some great girl talk. Or I can schedule some time with Whitney to go hiking or to a movie, which usually gets me out of my head and transports me into another reality. Or I can get together with Stephanie and discuss the troubles of the world, trading ideas and creative suggestions about work or kids. And, of course, I can reach out to my own children—never looking to them to fill the void of my loneliness—but to realize how fortunate I am to have my two amazing sons in my life.

Suddenly, I'm not feeling so lonely.

As I refined my style of verbal meditation over the years, I found I could very quickly get a Q & A dialogue by zeroing in on my own internal clarity. Instead of writing out my powerful questions at night, often I'd write them as part of my morning writing session. I'd write a question, I'd get an answer. I'd write another question, I'd get another answer. Occasionally, the tone of the response was so emphatic I felt compelled to write it out in all caps. I didn't even realize I was doing that at first, but it certainly got my attention. Other times, when I was being ridiculously hard on myself, my responses came as gentle jokes, making fun of me to see how seriously I was taking some small issue. As the answers I got led to real-world solutions that addressed my recurring life themes—how to reach out to a friend, how to build a team of professional advisors, how to build stronger relationships with my boys—you bet I began to pay close attention.

Whether it was the universe, God, or just me at my clearest focusing on solutions that worked for me made no difference. My life began to change. When I struggled with some problem and just plain forgot to ask for help in a simple and clear way, I didn't get the answer. Suddenly, I'd remember to ask and, sure enough, I'd get my answer. Amazing, you're saying? That's all it takes? There's only one way to find out—give it a try.

SUMMARY: REVERSING YOUR RECURRING THEMES

I didn't know anything about recognizing recurring life themes when I was a lonely teenager, let alone how to reverse them and find more positive patterns of behavior. The cumulative result of my father's emotional distance, my stepmother's iciness, and my mother's anger was that I learned to back away from my own emotions. None of the adults in my life knew how to show their love for me, although I don't doubt now that they actually did love me, so I felt unloveable and unworthy.

In this chapter, we've begun to recognize recurring life themes by looking at ourselves through literature, legend, and myth. By beginning to acknowledge those themes, we can begin to reverse them and replace the behavior that results from these negative themes with more positive results, as I did by learning that help was out there if I could learn to ask for it, or knowing that I could build a base of loving friends if I could unlearn the belief that I was meant to be alone. By mastering the simple but effective process of verbal meditation, we've added another tool to our arsenal of ways to link internal clarity and external action.

In chapter five, we'll start to shift our thinking from negative to positive by creating a credo, or personal motto, that reinforces who and what we truly want to be. We'll also see how dramatically you can change your perspective to change your life. We've all got our flaws. I'm not suggesting you should ignore them or neglect to work on them. We need to keep limiting self-beliefs in proper perspective. As the old song says, isn't it about time you began to accentuate the positive?

5

A Cult of One

Shifting Your Perspective from Limiting to Liberating

"Extreme hopes are born of extreme misery."
—**Bertrand Russell**

When a friend of a mine, a bright young woman of twenty-eight, was going through a particularly bad boyfriend time and chastising herself mercilessly for her supposed weakness, I told her my story about Thomas. In the next couple of chapters, I'll be telling you the story of the most debilitating relationship of my life and how it eventually became a turning point for me. I had to come to grips with the limiting life perspective I was allowing to shape the quality of my relationships and my life negatively.

In my twenties, I was too ashamed to tell anyone about the strangeness of my long-term affair with Thomas, even if I'd been able to understand it myself. I recognize that the weight of my family baggage combined with an inability to hear my inner voice had resulted in a devastating theme that

I played out in this humiliating and destructive romance. My deep-seated belief that I was fundamentally unworthy of success, love, and joy caused me to attract people into my life who systematically, intentionally, and repeatedly discounted my feelings and diminished my self-worth. Thomas was my rock bottom.

My relationship and subsequent break-up with Thomas taught me a great deal about perspective and how it can either limit or liberate you, depending on your point of view. In this chapter, we'll look at your perspective on the world and your place in it. Let's see how that delicate balance between your internal voice and your external world is affected by something entirely within your control: your own perspective.

PICKING YOUR PERSPECTIVE

In this chapter, we're going to talk about picking your perspective, because whether you realize it or not, it's up to you how you perceive the events that occur in your life. I'm not saying that you can control whether or not those events take place—you don't run the planet—but you can control how you perceive them. You know that old expression about the glass being either half empty or half full? I'm sure you know people who'd go with the half empty every time, right? And you probably also know some half fulls. Same glass, same amount of water, the only thing different is who's looking at the glass. That's perspective.

I think of perspective as a continuum, a range from empty to half empty to half full to full. Where are you on that continuum? Do you always go right to the worst-case scenario, the bleakest outlook on circumstances? Or maybe the worst possible self-belief you could choose? On the other hand, if you believe, as I do, that how you see the world is a matter of choice, then wouldn't you choose pleasure over pain, success over failure, fun over drudgery every time? In other words, wouldn't you rather be a half full than a half empty? You can be—if you pick the life perspective you want instead of letting it pick you.

As you go on to read about my experiences with Thomas, you'll see how failing to strive for internal clarity can translate into negative external action. If you are basing your life perspective on negative recurring themes rather than doing the internal homework required to turn those themes into positive ones, you're probably getting negative results. In this chapter, I'll give you some specific tools to help you change your perspective so you can accentuate the positive.

LIVING LIFE HALF EMPTY

When I told my friend how I had struggled through those years with Thomas, she was absolutely floored by my story, that someone as seemingly together as I was could have been so utterly self-destructive and desperate in the face of love. I assured her I was not the first strong woman, nor she the last, to lose perspective on life.

Of course, like most people who allow themselves to get stuck in a negative pattern, I was totally oblivious to my own choices. Oblivious to the fact that by choosing to be with Thomas, I was choosing to live life half empty. Later, I wondered why Thomas's claims that he could read my mind and commune with spirits were no stranger to me than his staying up all night or watching four television sets simultaneously. Without question, I accepted these unusual traits equally and thought I was being open-minded when, in fact, I was ignoring all the danger signs that were flashing right in front of me twenty-four hours a day.

Thomas came into my life when I was confused, lonely, and frantically seeking to reconnect with the soul I felt I was losing inch by inch. After having grown up with so little emotional support or guidance, I'd entered the adult world of work and responsibility utterly lacking in confidence. In vain, I tried church, I tried chanting, I tried drinking. None of these brought me much comfort or direction. When Thomas appeared with his unusual gifts, I let myself believe he was the answer, my spiritual guide, a messenger sent to right me on my path. And that's exactly what he became for me. Later. After I'd gained some much-needed perspective on why I'd spent almost six years in a relationship that brought me considerably more pain than it did joy.

When I first met Thomas, I thought he was dashing, handsome, and very mysterious. The talent agent for whom I worked told me that Thomas was a serious actor who also produced and directed independent films. If we only had more clients like him, he said, what a dream job his would be. I was in my early twenties, had just dropped out of grad school and moved to Los Angeles, and was working as a receptionist at a small talent agency, just upstairs from a stylish and famously expensive industry restaurant.

I longed to be an actress and probably was equal as far as looks and talent to any of the clients whose photos I pulled daily for the casting breakdowns—the Hollywood service to which pictures and résumés of actors were routinely submitted for various jobs around town. I had no real idea of how to go about getting started and was too scared or embarrassed to ask for help. The ultimate irony was that, once again, I had chosen to surround myself with people in a position to help me and yet instead of declaring my desire and getting on with it, I quietly submitted to a life of solitude and service, completely unnoticed by those who were doing precisely what I wanted to do.

It was my recurring Jane Eyre "I am subservient, I am alone, I am unloved" theme all over again. And on some unconscious level, I suppose Thomas was my Mr. Rochester.

Thomas called the agency one day—he had a deep, sonorous voice and I remember thinking I could listen to him talk for hours—asking if he could come by and borrow his industry reel, a videotape the agents used to showcase an actor's work. He wanted to make a copy as part of a film package he was putting together. I was thoroughly impressed. Thomas was one of those clients who rarely complained, frequently got work on his own, and always seemed to understand the realities of the business. In short, he was a relative rarity in entertainment: an actor who behaved like an adult and didn't have too many expectations of the people who were charged with securing him employment. I didn't discover until much later how little the work actually meant to him and that the appearance of cooperation was merely indifference.

Happy to accommodate his dream client, my boss searched the office tape library but couldn't find Thomas's tape. He asked me to call Thomas to let him know. I was not prepared to deliver even marginally bad news to the owner of that beautiful voice, so I undertook an all-out search of the cupboards and shelves until I found a three-quarter-inch tape-labeled simply THOMAS WATERS. When he came to retrieve the tape, Thomas asked me out to dinner and I immediately accepted, never giving a moment's thought to whether or not it was appropriate to go out with an agency client.

After I became a studio executive, I always marveled at those very young women, sometimes just out of college, who came in for interviews and were so completely self-assured. They wore the right clothes, said the right things, and almost always got the right jobs. They were women who had been taught by caring fathers about things like job interviews, buying stereo equipment, and watching out for men who only wanted one thing.

Those more knowing girls, with their Chanel bags and confident laughter, understood men better than I and were never surprised, much less flattered, when guys showered them with attention and begged for their favors. These young women expected attention from men, just as they had received it from loving fathers all their lives. I, on the other hand, was incredulous and grateful anytime a man focused any attention my way. It made me very easy prey.

From our first date, I was hooked and so was Thomas. He came to collect me one warm Saturday summer evening from the slightly shabby Hollywood apartment I shared with a friend from college. Although I was naïve in many ways, I was not without my little vanities. Knowing the pretty picture I presented, I was sitting on the floor surrounded by yards of chintz, sewing flowered curtains to cover the shades on our big living room picture window when Thomas arrived to pick me up for our dinner date. Although the task was a real one, the timing was sheer theatrics. I knew exactly what effect the classical guitar music and the soft lamp light on my long curls and little slip dress would have on him. Though not exactly an innocent, I was ill-equipped for the stormy six-year relationship that was to follow.

On that first date, we went to an old-fashioned neighborhood restaurant where we ate steak and drank red wine. Thomas told me that I looked like a young Elizabeth Taylor or Vivien Leigh with my long black hair and deep blue eyes. He swore he could sense the passion just beneath my cool surface, but doubted anyone else had ever noticed it before. Had I not been so intoxicated by the thought that someone might finally see me for my true self, I would have realized that my negative life perspective—that I was inherently unlovable and undeserving—was not allowing me to assess the situation accurately. In my desperation for connection, I failed to recognize his line for the very obvious come-on that it was. Not that he was lying, but similar to the scene of domesticity I'd staged for his arrival, he understood the art of embellishment.

After dinner, Thomas suggested we stop off at his director friend's house in the Valley nearby, just on the other side of Griffith Park from the restaurant. His friend was shooting a film in Africa, and Thomas had promised to water his plants and bring in his mail. If I saw the set-up for seduction coming, I ignored it. Soon, within just a couple of months, I had fit my entire life neatly into Thomas's, like a desert mouse carving a little nest into the arm of a cactus.

Thomas and I both perceived Thomas as the center of the universe. The truth was he was vain, narcissistic, lazy, and unkind. Somehow I managed to ignore all that and instead considered myself privileged to be part of his world. Never mind that his world included my putting my projects, timetable, and dreams aside for his. I did it not willingly but gleefully. He loved me, I told myself, and that was all that mattered.

As I looked back later, a series of burning questions arose: Who was that girl who threw those years away? How had I become so isolated and desperate that I altered my entire worldview to accommodate his? And how could I now shift my perspective to transform the shame of that intensely negative relationship into a positive life lesson?

Tool # 9: Change Your Perspective, Change Your Life

Can you think of a time when you felt stuck in your life? Maybe you knew what you were doing wasn't working, but you had no idea what to try or where to turn next in order to make a change. Maybe you were so overwhelmed with options that you shut down, unable to make any sort of move. With Thomas, I was stuck in the midst of the problem without any sense of direction. I couldn't have seen my way out if it had been right in front of me until a family crisis shook up my perspective. I don't want you to wait for a crisis in order to shift your perspective. So I designed this tool to help you get outside yourself in order to see yourself better.

Our general perspective on life is similar to the concept of recurring themes in that it tends to define who we are and influence our behavior. In our quest to change our external actions or behaviors, let's see if we can first alter our perspective. Once you've picked the perspective you want, it's much easier for the desired actions and outcomes to follow.

I want you to think of an image that epitomizes your general outlook or perspective on life. Maybe you're that Energizer bunny who just keeps going and going and going. It's not being the bunny that's important, it's how you feel about being that energetic bunny. Are you delighted to keep going and going and going? Is it fun being bouncy and pink and rolling along on those little wheels? Or is it draining the hell out of you to keep clanging those tiny cymbals without an opportunity to stop and rest? Knowing how you feel about the recurring themes in your life is what I mean by perspective. And once you get a handle on your perspective, you can shift it at will.

I used to picture myself as a rock-climber, moving toward the summit one finger- or toehold at a time. Swinging, struggling, grasping for the next grip; it was hard, sweaty work, even though I could see the top of the cliff just up above. That image played through my mind continually until I realized that I'd created it and—guess what?—I could change it. I decided to change that perspective and, instead, saw myself swinging my leg over the top of that summit and coasting downhill in a struggle-free glide that picked up momentum as I went. It was such a freeing experience that I want to teach you to identify your own limiting images and to then replace them with ones that liberate you, bringing relief, peace, and joy.

Here's what I want you to do:

1. Go to your relaxation spot and stretch out, close your eyes, and let all the tension drain out of you. Take a few deep breaths and let an image come to mind that sums up your perspective on yourself and your life. Maybe you envision yourself skydiving. Are you white-knuckling it all the way to the ground or thrilled with the rush of wind and your own victory over fear? Or maybe you picture yourself interviewing for your dream job. Does this image fill you with confidence or turn you into a monosyllabic moron?

2. Play with this image, give it an activity, and let a scene unfold. What are you doing? Is the scene active or passive? Fun or boring? How do you feel about this scenario? Is it pleasurable? Would you want to do it again? Never do it again?

3. Let your activity reach its natural conclusion and then open your eyes. Write a few lines about this visualization experience in your Traveling Hopefully Daybook. Make sure you describe the image and the activity. What does this scene say about your perspective on life?

4. Now that you've identified your perspective, let's think about shifting it. Can you alter your existing image and activity to give you an image that is more positive, more energizing, more loving? Like how I shifted my image from a sweaty rock climber to a breezy downhill glider? Or do

you need an entirely new image and activity to reflect the perspective you want to develop about your place in the world? Record your thoughts in your daybook.

Remember the story I told you in the last chapter about the script librarian? Clearly, she and I had two very different perspectives on my behavior. Same scenario, different perspectives. Although you might not be able to shift someone else's perspective, your change in perspective can often affect theirs. In other words, if I had seen myself as an open vessel letting help, knowledge, and support flood into me like the half-full glass, I would certainly have allowed her to help me pick my three monologues and maybe even direct my performance. If that openness to receiving help had been my perspective, I am sure she wouldn't have had the perspective that I was an "arrogant snot" (ouch!). Remember, you can't change other people's behavior so you must focus on picking your perspective and letting the subsequent external actions follow. The people in your life will respond positively or not, but at least you'll be moving forward, Traveling Hopefully by design instead of by default.

I'll give you another example from my illustrious academic career. When I was a theater major, one of my professors told me I needed to work on my voice to make it stronger for acting. He didn't tell me how or where to do this; I was on my own for that. I decided to go next door to the music department and sign up for an opera workshop. Every week, scared out of my wits, I got up at the front of the classroom and attempted to knock off a Bizet aria or Schumann art song. The truth is, I could barely warble a show tune, let alone an operatic piece, but I gave it the old college try.

Somehow I made it through the entire semester without once fainting or throwing up, or even forgetting my music. I made a C in the workshop. I was mortified. It took my GPA down a notch, but mostly it was the ego blow that was so painful. Was I destined to be a C singer? Did this mean I had a C acting voice? And was a C good, average, or bad? Harry Truman might have said that C students run the world, but to me, a C was dreadful, indicating I was untalented for having earned it. Only years later did I give myself credit for being a gutsy kid who was willing to infiltrate a very intimidating music department and attempt to sing opera, all because I wanted to be a better artist. It took me about twenty years to shift my perspective to see the courage behind that C. Better late than never, I tell myself now, which is also entirely a matter of perspective.

Ever notice that frequently we're harder on ourselves than anyone else is? No matter who dishes out what, we can beat them every time by being just a little more critical and a little less forgiving of ourselves. I think most people want to succeed, to achieve, to have great marriages, to raise happy kids, to enjoy their work. Often, we just don't know how to shift our perspectives to see our struggles as noble instead of futile, or our relationships as happy works in progress instead of battle grounds.

Learning to understand the power of perspective and your ability to shift it is another way to clear out the old baggage and head off on a new path. My story about Thomas dramatically illustrates that if we let our negative perspectives dictate our actions, we're destined to live out our negative life themes. If I had understood the process of Traveling Hopefully, I would never have gotten so deeply into the relationship with Thomas. Back then, my perspective that I was lucky to have anyone love me, regardless of how it made me feel, got me exactly what I envisioned. I had to go the long way around to get my life back on track but I don't want you to waste another second in getting everything you deserve in your life.

COMMUNICATING YOUR PERSPECTIVE

By the second night with Thomas, I found out why we had spent the first night at his friend's house and not his own. At age thirty-seven, Thomas lived at home with his mother and father. Or, as he would say, they lived with him. My refusal to pick up on that distinction was my very first but by no means my last leap of faith in his favor. In theater, they call it suspension of disbelief, and I had it in spades. In other words, I was not only able to ignore an ever-widening credibility gap, despite all sorts of ringing bells and swelling sirens, but instead imbued Thomas with a number of saintly qualities for taking care of his aging parents. Later, I saw that my lack of meaningful connection to my own family and my desire to fit somewhere, anywhere, clouded my perception beyond all reason.

We quickly fell into a routine of sorts. Since I had few friends and little contact with family, no one noticed, least of all me, that my life was spiraling out of control. Thomas rarely came to my apartment. Instead I would drive over to the house he shared with his parents in the San Fernando Valley, lugging my overnight bag since he didn't like me to leave anything behind. He said my apartment, though large and light-filled, depressed him and that my roommate's frenetic energy disturbed him. We spent most of our free time hanging out in his den, watching sports (him) or old movies (me) on the bank of side-by-side televisions that were on all hours of the day and most of the night. Thomas was happiest, if such a word could ever be applied to him, in his pajamas, ordering dinner in, calling his bookie, and betting on anything that moved.

Once in a while we went out to a movie or restaurant, but only at off-times when there weren't many people around and the vibes wouldn't bother him too much. He couldn't stand crowds, picking up people's thoughts and being assaulted by their negativity, he claimed. Never mind that he loved going to the racetrack, regardless of the time of day or size of the crowd. It was a lark at first, buying tickets for the fancy clubhouse section of the track, watching the beautiful, high-strung horses burst out of their paddocks and race as if they understood full well that people were counting on them. I quickly learned the rules of the game—how to read a racing form, how to place my bets, and where Thomas liked to stand so he could get the clearest messages from his spirit friends. He said he could tell which horses would be running well just by looking at them and by picking up vibrations from the racing form itself. As crazy as it sounded, I watched him pick six winners in a row on several occasions and four or five winners out of six on many occasions, feats that didn't specifically defy the odds but certainly stretched them to their limits. When he asked me to claim the pick-six winnings for him—which had to be signed for at a special window and then reported to the IRS—so it would go on my income tax records and not his, I barely batted an eye. When he won, he always gave me a portion of the winnings, and I came to expect it, like a prostitute accustomed to picking up her hundred off the dresser.

Within weeks, everything was about Thomas. His needs seemed so much more important than everyone else's, especially mine, that I found it surprisingly easy to tailor my life to fit his. Thomas had been a television star in his late teens, appearing on one of the first big prime time soap operas, until his character ran its course and he found himself looking for work for the first time in his youthful career. Handsome and muscular, with sandy blond hair and deep brown eyes, his image of soulfulness and depth reminded audiences and critics of James Dean, and he definitely looked like a rising star.

Thomas made the fatal choice of refusing to continue on in television, preferring to hold out for feature films rather than sign on for the starring role in another prime time series that later became a huge hit. At that time, there was still a chasm between TV and movie actors that was difficult to span. Just as he bet on his racehorses only to win but never to place or show, Thomas bet everything on a feature film career and lost.

Not willing to concede without a fight, he began to write and produce vehicles for himself and made a couple of decent, minor films which showcased him nicely but never took off commercially. Still, I was in awe of his accomplishments and single-minded focus and firmly believed that everything would change for him, and so for me, in the blink of an eye, just as he claimed. In the meantime, as my youth and looks and opportunities slipped by, I would be content to be his muse, his silent partner.

Eventually, I quit the talent agency since the regular hours made me too unavailable should Thomas need me either for a project or playtime. I typed his scripts, did a rewrite once in a while, and generally kept his life on track. Meantime, I booked an occasional commercial or modeling job, although I lacked the confidence and the contacts to make a serious run at an acting career. Mostly, I worked as a temp at the various studios around town, faking my way through, picking up skills here and there, and learning a bit about the entertainment industry.

A year into our relationship, I had no job, no money, no friends, and no continuous contact with my family. Little wonder that I held such a skewed sense of reality; I had no touchstone or frame of reference for what might have been worthwhile or even appropriate pursuits for someone like me. Not that I would have believed that there was a benchmark or standard by which to compare my life. I'd already succumbed to a cultlike mentality, albeit a cult of one, and refused to believe that other people's lives had any relevance to mine.

At the time, I was barely even aware of the negative messages I was constantly bombarding myself with, messages like "You're just lucky you've got someone in your life" and "Don't rock the boat." Without even realizing the self-sabotage in which I was indulging, I continued to sustain myself on a diet rich in negativity. And when this negativity had become so pervasive that it became my life perspective and I had nearly shut out all ability to hear the positive anymore, a tragedy occurred that would make me change the way I thought about—and talked to—myself.

Tool # 10: Creating Your Credo

Even as you're reading this, are you aware of the fact that you've got a constant monologue going in your head? Stop right now and listen in for a minute. What are you thinking about as you read the words on the page? Maybe you're thinking about my story, or about what the title of Tool #10 says to you, or maybe what you want to have for dinner. Whatever it is, I want you to hear that monologue loud and clear, because that inner voice is always yakking at you.

We've all heard the terms self-talk, inner critic, internal monologue. No matter how noisy your environment or communicative your friends and family, you talk to yourself more than anyone else talks to you. Ever. So you better be saying some good things. Messages to yourself are like perspective; it's up to you to pick them, so you might as well make them positive.

Now that you're learning to turn up the volume on your inner voice, it's time to understand that you can also program it to say the right things to you—things that inspire you to achieve, motivate you to act, incite you to risk, force you to conquer fear, convince you to love. All of those behaviors are within your control; it's just a matter of learning to program the positive messages you send to yourself, rather than hoping that by some miracle you might say something encouraging to yourself. After all, why would you leave such important messages to chance?

Do you remember the quirky television drama *Ally McBeal*, about a group of hipper than hip young attorneys? Okay, the lawyer girls' skirts were a tad short and everyone shared one unisex bathroom, but there were some really interesting social comments about who those characters were and how they fit into society. Ally was, of course, famously neurotic and had an even more neurotic therapist, played brilliantly by Tracey Ullman. As crazy as most of her advice was, one thing Tracey encouraged her client to try was really insightful; she made Ally pick a theme song for herself. Dr. Tracey had Ally literally choose a song and sing it in her head over and over again until the message began to seep into her unconscious and help her to change her outward behavior.

All right, calm down. I'm not going to suggest you burst into song—unless of course that's your particular passion, and then by all means, sing your heart out—but I want you to incorporate that kind of thinking into your change of perspective. That is, the idea that you can have a personal theme song or mantra, which is the Hindu term for a word or invocation that is repeated in prayer, that carries an important message for your life. Let's proceed with selecting that slogan, what I call creating your credo. You've already learned about picking your perspective, that is, your ability to shift to a more positive attitude about the events or emotions you're experiencing. Now you're going to create a credo that communicates that perspective.

Let me give you a couple of examples of credos I've created in my life, both limiting and liberating. By now I think you've gotten a pretty clear picture that I can be driven and, at my worst, a workhorse convinced that I'm in harness and pulling the plow all by myself. On second thought, let's ditch the farm animal metaphors and return to the Jane Eyre imagery. I work hard, I seldom ask for help, I don't have a lot of fun. Yecch, right? Well, I had a credo back then, and as I review it today, it's no wonder that I was signing myself up for a life of drudgery. Here was my credo back then, in my Jane Eyre the-put-upon-governess days: "I will not die on this plateau." That's what I frequently and routinely repeated to myself, "I will not die on this plateau." All right, so it did keep me trudging forward one foot in front of the other, but it was brutal, bleak, and joyless. It also made me feel like disaster was just around every corner, assuming plateaus even have corners. I was convinced I'd better keep moving despite my pain/exhaustion/loneliness or I might keel over and die of frostbite or heatstroke right out there on that plateau with the summit just feet away.

No wonder I was so worn out all the time with that image constantly playing in my head. Finally, I'd had enough. Which, by the way, is when you start to change: when you can't stand not to change, or as the famed philosopher Bertrand Russell wrote, "Extreme hopes are born of extreme misery." If your personal credo is adding to your misery, change it. Like your perspective, you pick it, so you might as well make it joyful and inspiring. When I finally figured out that, once again, I had created this little slice of hell but I could alter it, I created a new credo. Now it's "Maximum enthusiasm, minimum effort." Remember my downhill glider easing through life? That's maximum enthusiasm with a whole lot less effort than I was used to expending. It's also a lot less lonely and a lot more fun.

Additional credos (you can have more than one, of course) that have reflected perspective shifts for me include moving from the risk-averse "Err on the side of caution," to the much more freeing but admittedly riskier "Err on the side of action." My former assistant, Michaela, who was a master at bringing out the best in me, used to repeat her credo frequently as a not-so-subtle reminder when she felt I needed to restrain myself for some of my more conservative clients. Once you get her sing-song credo in your head, it's hard to let go: "Dignity and grace and a smile on your face." Whenever she said it, it did make me smile, and it always reminded me to act like a lady, even if I was ready to attack. Her handwritten note proclaiming this credo is still posted above my desk.

Here are some examples of credos that people have shared with me to help jumpstart your thinking before you create your own credo.

EXAMPLES OF CREDOS

Keep your eyes on the prize.

Strong and centered.

Pick your battles.

Whatever it takes.

You have to be able to look at yourself in the mirror.

Take no prisoners.

Love is an action.

Now it's time for you to create your credo. Don't agonize over this. If it sounds like what my kids call "torturement," be sure to add a little fun to your credo. As you know, I think fun is highly underrated. Here's what I want you to do:

1. Sit down with your Traveling Hopefully Daybook and take a few deep breaths. Let your mind start to play with the idea of creating your credo.

2. Now think of a saying that feels like an appropriate credo for your life. It can be a well-known quote, an old expression, or a phrase that you make up yourself—as long as it represents you and your perspective on life. Write it out in your daybook. If you want to list a couple of credos, go right ahead.

3. Now take a good look at the credo or credos you wrote down. Read them out loud. How do they make you feel? Do they make you tired? Do they make you smile? Does your credo inspire you to get up and move or make you want to lie down and take a nap? Remember, the only right and wrong is what works for you.

4. You can also try incorporating the practice of creating your credo into your verbal meditations and seeing what comes up for you as you write each morning in your Traveling Hopefully Daybook. Keep experimenting and change your credo as often as necessary, until it feels like an accurate communication of your perspective, or the perspective you're working to develop. You'll know when it's right.

5. Now incorporate your credo into your life. Repeat it to yourself when you need a pep talk or a reminder. Share it with someone else when you think they might benefit from

its wisdom or spirit, or when you think it can be an aid in explaining how you tick.

In the course of teaching and speaking about the concept of Traveling Hopefully, I've discovered that the credos people choose for themselves—from "Do it naturally" to "Pick your battles wisely" to "Love is an action"—are generally quite reflective of who they are. And not always to their benefit. How would you like to be the man (or wife or kids of the man) who told me that "Life's a bitch and then you die" was his personal credo? You pick the perspective—and the credo that communicates it—so you might as well make both of them inspiring and positive. Maybe the "life's a bitch" guy is due for a credo change.

SUMMARY: MISERY LOVES A SHIFT IN PERSPECTIVE

Back in my Thomas years, I chose a self-defeating, joyless, painful perspective that reflected my negative life themes. I chose it, and I lived it. It took my stepmother's suicide to wake me up to the truth that my life perspective wasn't acceptable any longer. In this chapter, we've seen that it is solely your perception of events, not the events themselves, that provides you with your perspective on life. All the way back to your childhood dramas and your childhood dreams, it's your interpretation that counts. You can throw in the towel and exclaim "poor me" or you can choose to trump the hand that life has dealt you by sending yourself the message that how you choose to live your life is up to you. Picking your perspective and creating a credo that reflects and communicates it can give you the inspiration to start Traveling Hopefully— right this minute.

In chapter six, we'll set off on the Trail of Tears. I'll take you deeper into the catastrophic circumstances surrounding my stepmother Fran's death and my subsequent break-up with Thomas, which was also the breakthrough that finally allowed me to go beyond my own limits and move toward inner freedom.

6

Trail of Tears

Facing Flaws, Embracing Imperfection, and Risking Vulnerability

"Where there's life, there's hope."

—Terence

My great-great-grandmother Nancy Hunter was a Cherokee woman married to my mother's great-grandfather. My mother remembers Nancy silently moving around the kitchen, her dark hair worn Indian-style in a long braid down her back. Although I never knew my great-great-grandmother, sometimes I think I sense her spirit hovering nearby, watching over me like a guardian angel.

The Cherokee believe our world is based on a flow of interconnected energy, which is constantly moving in circular motions throughout the universe. The medicine wheel is the ancient symbol of the Cherokee, representing that sacred circle of life with its four directions, each coinciding with a different aspect of being.

East is spirit, south is natural environment, west is body, and north is mind. Long before Western medicine recognized the importance of the mind-body connection and the interrelated healing techniques which are becoming more and more prevalent today, the Cherokee and other ancient people instinctively understood our need for balance and harmony. When we strike the harmonic balance that is right for us, life works. When we fail to find that balance, depression, disease, and dissatisfaction result.

While the Cherokee elders might not have used my term "Traveling Hopefully," I have no doubt that they would embrace the concept. Traveling Hopefully is all about finding a balance that works for you.

Transforming your life to be more positive and joyful is not always an easy task. As you've discovered, positive change requires that you do the internal homework, then take the crucial steps toward external action. Transformation also requires healthy doses of self-acceptance and self-compassion. Though you may have plenty of compassion for other people, even total strangers, have you considered how much compassion you have for yourself? In this chapter, we'll look at the power of facing your flaws, embracing imperfection, and risking vulnerability, as well as the potentially disastrous results of failing to do so. Ironically, it was my stepmother's tragic inability to find harmony in her life that drove me finally to break off my affair with Thomas and begin the journey of Traveling Hopefully.

As my relationship with Thomas stretched into five torturous years, it began to dawn on me that all the goals I had for my life—creative work, international travel, satisfying relationships—were not only unrealized but seemingly unreachable. When I was in my late twenties, doubts about Thomas started to bubble up to the surface. For all his mysticism, I'd begun to realize that he wasn't a good person. I saw now that he was a racist, that he lacked ethics in business, and that he was often downright spooky when it came to his psychic gifts. Instead of being a generous teacher, magnanimous with his spiritual knowledge and eager to share, he was either just plain stingy or afraid of blowing his showmanlike cover. Whatever secrets I'd hoped to learn from him, he was not giving them up at any cost.

And yet, I clung stubbornly to the notion that he was the most important thing in my world. My recurring life theme of unworthiness had led me to believe that I was lucky to have anyone in my life, no matter how I was treated or what I got out of the relationship. That flame inside me, that ever-present spirit that wouldn't let go no matter how hard I tried to ignore it, still flickered. I could still catch the fire of a dream that wouldn't die, a vision of a very different life. Of children, a home, a fulfilling career, a loving partnership, a dog on the front lawn, all things that seemed so alien that I wondered if they could exist for me. At the time, I thought not.

Instead, I focused on a dream that was more accessible, my goal of going to Europe. As much as I feared admitting it to Thomas, I felt my life was passing me by, and I was intent on traveling to the great capitals—London, Paris, Rome—with or without him. Thomas, eleven years my senior, had already seen and done many of the things I longed to do, but seemed to have little need to help me fulfill my dreams. I was on my own. Timidly, I stated my desire. To my surprise, he decided he would go with me, not so much because he wanted to, but because he was jealous of anything or anyone that might compete for my attention, even a city.

So at the age of twenty-eight, after scrimping and saving and running up all my credit cards, I booked the cheapest flights and hotels I could find, and we set off to Europe. I'd been all over Asia, through much of Mexico and Canada, and was no stranger to travel, but this trip was different. It was something I wanted to do, insisted on doing, in fact, a bit of that flame refusing to be extinguished. It was exciting, a little dangerous with Thomas in tow. He was unpredictable and moody, at first going along with me to all the tourist sights but increasingly sour about getting up early, eating unfamiliar food, walking for miles — precisely the things that I found so stimulating. I was beginning to feel alive and to notice that he put a damper on my enthusiasm and made me doubt every decision I made and every interest I had.

Finally, in Paris, which was the most exquisite city I'd ever seen, it hit me that despite his ongoing complaints about my many imperfections, it was Thomas who was so deeply flawed, not me. Having dinner one night in a little bistro, I commented nonchalantly that a man seated nearby resembled a certain movie star. That was it for Thomas. He was convinced that I wanted to sleep with the man and he with me, that we were exchanging thoughts and mentally arranging some clandestine meeting, and Thomas would not stand for it. He left the restaurant in a huff, and I sat in humiliated silence, not knowing where to look or what to say.

After we returned from Europe, things got worse. Thomas flipped back and forth between abject admiration and utter disdain for me. He was constantly pointing out my faults, sometimes accurately, sometimes not. Under this constant barrage of criticism, I finally realized the irony of his double standard. While his flaws were written off as artistic temperament, mine were inexcusable imperfections. In his way of thinking I was not entitled to have any flaws, real or imagined. A vicious cycle developed. As I became more withdrawn, he became more extreme. I never knew what to expect or how to please him. If we were in a public place and someone looked at me, I would glance away for fear it would anger him. If someone spoke to me, I would answer politely without inviting further conversation. If we were driving down the street and I saw a man jogging, I would avert my eyes, convinced a stray thought about him might cross my mind and Thomas would pick it up and berate me as flirtatious, disloyal, and shallow. Finally I began to sing in my head, an endless droning hum all the time, because I had come to believe it was the only way I could keep Thomas from reading my mind.

What had happened to me? I was not some raving maniac. I was a bright, attractive, college-educated woman with talent and promise, and yet here I was, singing to myself to drown out the mind probe I was sure was happening without my consent. I had no idea where to turn. I might have approached one of the few friends I'd kept in touch with since I met Thomas, but I was afraid I would appear weak or even pathetic in their eyes. Only later, when I'd reached the crisis stage, was I willing to risk asking for the help I so desperately needed.

Somehow the time got away from me and before I knew it, I had devoted almost six years of my life to my relationship with Thomas. By the time we split up, my roommate had moved into a beautiful rent-controlled apartment near the beach that I had turned down because Thomas thought it was too far from his house. Thomas and I never discussed getting a place together, nor did he ever suggest I move in with him. I stayed in my apartment by myself although it was bigger than I needed and more expensive than I could afford. I was barely hanging on financially, continuing to do temporary office work with a few acting or modeling jobs sprinkled in.

Eventually, I began thinking about getting a full-time job, although Thomas constantly reminded me I had no skills and that no one who would want to hire me. I wanted a "creative" job, in which I would contribute to the development of film or television projects. During my temping years, after I had abandoned all hope of becoming an actress, that was the only type of full-time job I desired, but I found every means available to sabotage myself. I wondered why was it so simple for other people to have what they wanted when it seemed every desire I had was thwarted. I didn't understand then how my negative life themes were making positive action impossible. I knew nothing about internal clarity, about having a clear vision that could be translated into real-world external action. Instead, every desire I had was clouded with fear, riddled with self-doubt. No wonder I always took the supporting part, Jane Eyre–like, leaving others to their starring roles.

After ricocheting back and forth between little production companies and big studios, where I was either underqualified or overqualified, I was offered a job in the publicity department of a midsize television company that had been founded by the legendary Norman Lear. I had no concept what public relations was all about, but the head of the department was energetic and bright and assured me that if I did a good job, I would have a rosy future under his tutelage. At that time, I was temping in the finance department of a major studio. When my temporary boss found out about my job offer, he immediately countered and I found myself in the unlikely position of having people fight over me. Having leverage was a new concept for me, but I instinctively understood that this was my chance. I accepted the publicity job, setting a record for the highest starting wage ever paid to a new assistant. Although Thomas constantly made me doubt myself, there were external indicators that I did, indeed, have value.

On the day before I was to begin my new job, the first real, full-time, grown-up position I'd ever held in the entertainment industry, I came home to find a message on the answering machine from my father. My dad had only called me about three or four times in my entire life. He sounded upset, but the message was so garbled I couldn't catch what he was saying and, since it was late, I decided I would return the call in the morning. Hours later, about three A.M., Dad called again, and this time it was all too clear. My stepmother, Fran, had died and, I gathered, not from natural causes. The police had been in and out, Dad told me through what seemed to be a drunken or drug-induced haze, and he himself had not yet been ruled out as a suspect. I knew my father hadn't killed Fran. No one had to tell me she'd taken her own life.

Tool # 11: Facing Your Flaws and Embracing Imperfection

Fran's failure to find emotional harmony resulted in tragedy. From the outside, she had it all. A husband who adored her, a beautiful home, physical health, plenty of money. On the inside, she lacked acceptance and compassion for herself. Without those, there was no hope for inner peace.

Although Fran's death is an extreme example, we've all felt the painful effects of our own lack of self-acceptance at some point in our lives. We've all beaten ourselves up about our faults, relentlessly criticized and punished ourselves for our shortcomings. You might as well face it. Life is not perfect, and neither are you. Just by virtue of being a living, breathing human being, you are by definition a flawed creature. You can either face it or fight it.

In the following exercises, you'll see how facing your flaws and embracing imperfection can be significant steps toward making positive change as well as a huge relief. Wouldn't it be nice to feel as if you didn't have the weight of the world on your shoulders, if only for a few minutes each day? Don't think that facing your flaws and embracing imperfection means abdicating responsibility, quite the contrary. It means that you start to assess your shortcomings—realistically—then learn to balance self-criticism with self-acceptance, even as you're working toward solutions.

Facing your flaws requires that you identify the character traits in yourself that you feel don't measure up to your standards, or that you wish were different. If you can't put your finger on some of your more glaring faults, just ask around. Trust me, either your spouse, your colleagues, your friends, or family members will be all too happy to help you identify your least attractive traits. But I have to warn you: Don't ask unless you're ready to hear what they have to say.

Not to worry, you're not in this alone. There's a whole, big imperfect universe out there to keep you company. Though the concept of embracing imperfection is about accepting the world—and your role in it—as it is, not as you want it to be, it's also about loosening up on your own expectations. You need to understand that your actions can sometimes be less than perfect. Since all things are not created equal, you don't have to approach every workout, office task, or home improvement project as if it's the big one.

While most of us understand that some things, like parenting and romance, will never be perfect because human beings are inherently flawed, many of us expect the activities in which we regularly engage to hit that high-water mark. But how realistic is it—and how much do we really care—to tackle every tennis game or home repair job aiming for perfection? We're so desperate to be perfect that we've forgotten to strive for excellence, which is infinitely more attainable. I'm not saying that you, or those upon whom you rely for services or support, should never strive for perfection. Certainly, I'd expect perfection in my brain surgeon and tax preparer. But it's not essential to give every endeavor the same weight or importance. Once you realize that you can set realistic expectations and priorities, including picking some areas in which you don't need to be perfect, life just gets easier.

Cut yourself some slack and let's focus on flaws for a minute. Just in case you can't put your finger on any of yours at the moment, here's a list to help you out. See if any of these sound like you.

FLAWS AND FAULTS

Arrogance

Selfishness

Overcontrolling

Stinginess

Compulsiveness

Grudge-holding

Unforgiving

Paranoia

Bitterness

Lack of ambition or motivation

Anger

Depression

Lethargy

Emotional distance

Inability to communicate

Jealousy

Lack of integrity

Laziness

Fear

Lack of confidence

Lack of empathy

Naïveté or overtrusting

Condescension

Bullying

Manipulativeness

Duplicity

Greed

Procrastination

Lack of focus

Indecisiveness

Close-mindedness

Bigotry

Inability to manage stress

Self-loathing

Here's what I want you to do:

IDENTIFYING YOUR FIVE PRIMARY FLAWS

1. Make a list in your Traveling Hopefully Daybook of what you consider your five primary flaws. It doesn't matter whether or not these are traits that you believe you can change; we'll get to that a little later in this chapter. Your list of flaws can include character traits like chronic lateness, bad temper, reckless behavior, lack of confidence, loss of control, shyness, moodiness, etc.

2. Now, to get some realistic perspective, look at the items on your list. Rank them on a 1–10 scale as to how problematic each trait really is for you; that is, how much concern you have over each flaw you listed. A one means that that flaw is the least problematic, a ten is most problematic. Don't consider whether or not your flaws are problematic for others, unless their being a problem for someone else makes them a problem for you.

My list of imperfections, and their rankings, looks like this:

1. Tend to withdraw or hold back when uncertain —7
2. Let problems reach a boiling point rather than articulating while still manageable —8
3. Avoid confrontation —6
4. Extremely self-critical —6
5. Overly ambitious —5

Maybe you've never really thought about your flaws before, or maybe it's all you ever think about. Writing them down forces you to face your flaws as well as your feelings about them. Look back at chapter one and see if any of these flaws tie into your family baggage, or chapter four to see if they fit somehow into your recurring life themes. As you begin facing your flaws, think about combining your awareness with acceptance so you can move toward correcting your flaws or, at least, making peace with them.

Let's go a step further and check out your perspective on perfection. In my work, I encounter a lot of overachievers. Many of them couldn't slack off if their lives depended on it. Even when they know intellectually that letting up on themselves, by going on vacation, exercising, or just taking a nap or reading a book every now and then, could result in recharging their business batteries or creative juices, they apply the same level of expectation and energy to almost all of their endeavors. Being less than superhuman, no matter how talented or driven they are, the result for their efforts is often disappointment or a sense of failure since they applied equal standards of perfection to unequal activities or events. Whew, are you as exhausted as I am?

On the other hand, you might be one of those people who capitalizes on the inability to do something perfectly as an excuse not to do it all. I'll give you an example from my life to which I'll bet plenty of you can relate. I recognize that I need to exercise but I'm not one of those people who loves to exercise. And I'm a busy person, like many of you. It's always been pretty easy to convince myself that until I had the luxury of enough time to get on a comprehensive daily workout program, it just wasn't worth getting started, because it's better not to exercise at all than to do it halfheartedly, right? Wrong!

The truth is that, for me, exercising twenty minutes a day, three days a week, is a whole lot better than not exercising at all. I was looking at my exercise program with an eye toward perfection, that is a five-day-a-week workout with a trainer as my standard, and I used that as my excuse. Once I embraced imperfection and appreciated the value of an imperfect exercise routine, I started working out. Twenty minutes, three days a week. Occasionally, I even get in a full hour. When I don't, I don't deprive myself of my twenty-minute workout, or even ten if that's all I have. This isn't brain surgery, this is a workout, and, in this case, something really is better than nothing.

Whenever I address writers' groups, there are invariably people with wonderful stories that would make wonderful books. Yet so many potential writers insist on not writing until they can find the freedom, focus, or flexibility to write perfectly. Which means, of course, that they may never pick up a pen or sit down in front of the computer. Unless they are willing to write badly, I tell them, they will never write well. The willingness to embrace imperfection will allow you to take the risk to write imperfectly, which is, of course, the beginning of writing well. Or writing at all. Try the following exercise to see if you can identify areas in which you need to strive for perfection and those for which it's just not that important.

RECOGNIZING WHEN YOU NEED TO STRIVE FOR PERFECTION AND WHEN YOU DON'T

1. In your daybook, make a list of five key projects you're working on right now or that you'd like to start. Your list can include tasks or projects related to parenting, fitness, work, home, or relationships.

2. Now prioritize these items on a 1–5 scale, with one applying to the item most worthy of striving for perfection, five the least. How does that feel? Are you surprised at your priorities? Was it difficult to rank them? Did you feel you wanted everything to be perfect? Is it a relief that you could identify something as a five on your perfection priority scale?

3. Next, make a list of the key items that you overemphasize, overstress, or overstrive for perfection on more than the task really justifies. In other words, do you really care how organized your sock drawer is? How clean your garage is? How neatly typed your phone list is? How does your list of less important projects make you feel? Is there anything you could just cross off forever?

4. Now that you've discovered that your flaws are not insurmountable and that not all tasks require perfection—go
   take a break. You've earned it.

CROSSING OVER TO COMPASSION

Accepting our imperfections, flaws, and faults is not an easy
thing to do. It takes courage and persistence, but it is far better than the alternative—to be wracked with self-doubt or,
worse, self-loathing. Perhaps if my stepmother had treated
herself with more compassion, her life would not have ended
as it did.

I called my new boss the day I was to begin my first studio
job to inform him of the death in my family and to let him
know I would need to start work a week later. Although I
managed to visit my family in Florida every couple of years,
it was relatively rare for them to visit me in California. I flew
back to Tampa to plan a funeral and clean out closets. This
was, of course, an enormous inconvenience for Thomas. Even
after five years together, he'd never met any of my family and
certainly didn't want to start under these sloppy circumstances. I handled what needed to be handled—family, funeral, canceling of magazine subscriptions—and returned
home to start my job the following week. It was late October,
almost the start of the holiday season, always an especially
bad time for my father, having lost my brother David at
Christmas. I knew how difficult it would be for Dad, so I invited him to stay with me for several weeks through Christmas and the New Year.

From the moment I picked him up at the airport, I saw
a completely changed man. Gone was the strong façade.
Gone the macho Southern gentleman. Overnight, he had
turned into this needy old person who was content to sit in

front of my television and watch sports and drink beer, something I'd never seen him do even once in my lifetime. I'd never seen him allow another person to take care of him, either, least of all me. But that's precisely what I found myself doing.

In the meantime, I was trying desperately to make it all up to Thomas. I was sorry my stepmother had done this bothersome thing, sorry my father was now such a burden, sorry I was working a full-time job. So I would just have to make it up somehow. More attention, more home-cooked meals, more sex. Whatever would make Thomas happy, I would attempt to do. Only now, I was slowly breaking down. Even I could see it.

After about three weeks, it was finally too much even for me, an expert in suffering, to take care of Thomas and Dad, so I shipped my father home, promising to come visit very soon. And I was left to face myself. But that was far too painful. Instead I worked. I volunteered for overtime, took on whatever projects no one else wanted, got in early, and left late. The need to avoid myself, my feelings, and my problems made me a wonderful employee. Although more socially acceptable than drugs or alcohol, obsessive workaholism still kept me from facing me. Until I received the mink coat and couldn't avoid me any longer.

Since my father was still alive, everything Fran owned at the time of her death went to him automatically. With his blessing, I gave most of it, including a couple of extravagantly expensive suits entirely unsuitable in the Florida humidity, to his housekeeper Marianne, who now had the distinction of representing the longest-term relationship in my father's life, other than me, since my siblings had severed their ties with Dad. Dad wanted me to have Fran's beloved mink coat with its little mink-lined matching hood. It was a

very dramatic ensemble, just like Fran. Even if my con-
science had allowed me to wear fur, where would a young
woman like me wear such a coat in southern California?

I decided to sell the mink. At that point, even though I had
a job, I was still deep in debt and every bit would help. In an
uncharacteristic display of gallantry, Thomas said he did not
want strangers coming into my apartment and he volunteered to put the mink up for sale. Only he didn't. It hung in
his closet for days, then weeks, until finally, when it became
clear to me that he had no intention of lifting a finger, I removed it from his closet and took it home to hang in mine.

Something about the mink sent me over the edge. It was
such a frivolous item, so unnecessary, so cruel yet at the same
time so luxurious and feminine. It made me think of Zelda
Fitzgerald or Greta Garbo. Or Fran. It was exactly her kind
of thing, beautiful and dramatic and glamorous and superfi-
cial. Now it was in my closet, and I hadn't a clue how to get
rid of it. I had thought Thomas would do this one thing for
me, especially since he didn't want strangers in my house.
Now he apparently no longer cared; gun-toting, knife-wielding
strangers were free to come and go at any hour of the day
or night. He had abandoned me, and I was at the end of
my rope.

It wasn't so much the mink. I could have given it to Good-
will, assuming the needy would want it, and taken a tax
write-off had I been so inclined. It was the abandonment.
Not that Thomas was ever particularly protective, but now,
when I needed him so badly, he was nowhere to be found.
I couldn't handle the financial pressure, my stepmother's suicide, my father's breakdown, or the sale of this ridiculous ex-
travagant coat that hung in my closet like some furry corpse.
After five years, I'd asked for one thing, and Thomas had let
me down. I was distraught. Broken.

I went into the kitchen and poured myself a glass of brandy. I rarely drank anything other than an occasional glass of wine, but I poured a big glassful and drank it down. There was no way I would call Thomas, I had no friends. I had no idea what to do. I was defeated.

I went to the closet and looked at the mink. I had yet to try it on; something about that act seemed so decadent, so wrong to me at that moment. But now I couldn't resist the impulse. I took it out of the closet, peeled off the waxy paper that was protecting it, from what I don't know, and slipped it on. The softness of that skin on mine was incredible. It had such a weight to it, I wondered how many animals it took to make one coat for one vain dead woman. I put it on, and like a wave, the sadness and despair just washed through me. In that moment, I realized how much I had wanted Fran to love me like a mother, as my own mother could not. My mother's heart held so much rage and bitterness, she would never have room for love. And Fran's held so much pain, she would never understand love's healing power.

Not sure my knees would hold, I sank to the ground and looked for refuge. Like a small wounded animal, like a mink perhaps, I crawled out of my room, too big, too open, too dangerous, and looked for something more cavelike. I came to rest in the central hallway of our apartment, an old-fashioned hall with a telephone nook and built-in linen cupboard. It was in the middle of the apartment, between the two bedrooms and the bath. Protected, without windows, access, or sunlight. Safer there, I lay down, the mink still wrapped around me, and drank, hoping I would somehow sink into oblivion; a mindless state of numbness. But I didn't. I began to cry and cry and every sob felt like a blow.

I cried until I thought my body must be covered with black and blue marks, convinced my anguish must show on the outside the way it felt on the inside. I wished someone would see the pain I felt. But I was afraid. Afraid to say who I was, what I felt, what I had become. I lay on the floor, maybe for hours, maybe for days, and asked for help, for someone or something to show me how to survive, until I felt a presence. It wasn't like those angel stories you read about in *People* magazine. It was just a feeling, yet so profound and unmistakable that I had no doubt that it was real.

I'm sure it was Fran who came to visit me, to deliver the message that everything was going to be okay. I smelled her perfume, the L'Air du Temps she always wore. I felt her presence, and then I felt her arms reach into the sleeves of that mink coat, her mink coat, and even though I never moved from my hard little curled-up knot on the floor, I felt her arms reach around me right through the coat, hugging me, holding me, and I knew there was a better way, and I would find it.

The next day, I opened the Yellow Pages and found a therapist who accepted payment on a sliding scale. This woman, whom I only saw for one critical month, saved my life and became just one of my army of supporters who set me upright and showed me the path that was in front of me all the time. When I told her how scared I was to be there, that I was sure Thomas intuited what I was doing even though I hadn't told him, she knew instantly that I was in deep trouble.

With her care and guidance, I swiftly extricated myself from that relationship. I did not pretend that I was cured or completed, that I had even begun to climb the enormous mountain of my pain and fear. That therapist and my own little stab at courage gave me a first step, one step only, but with a foot in the right direction, I finally began to make my way through the maze of past hurts, Traveling Hopefully toward acceptance.

Tool # 12: Vulnerability Is Power

I was at the height of my vulnerability as I lay on the floor of that hallway wrapped in my dead stepmother's mink coat. Even though I did not understand then that vulnerability is power, I knew instinctively that I had to take action or be consumed by my pain. Traveling Hopefully means finding the courage to take those positive steps forward despite seemingly insurmountable obstacles and crippling self-doubts. That devastating day stands out clearly in my memory as a shift in my personal energy field. That day was, for me, the breakthrough experience enabling me to overcome self-doubt and discover self-compassion. Once you've discovered acceptance and compassion for yourself, it is much easier to walk through your fears and risk being vulnerable.

THE CROSSOVER TO SELF-COMPASSION

Recognizing your flaws and understanding that you often give them more attention than they deserve can be the first step to treating yourself with greater tolerance and compassion. We're going to take the idea of self-acceptance a little deeper and see if you can begin to lighten the load of some of the flaws that are weighing on you. Here's what I want you to do:

1. Look back at your list of flaws, starting with the one that is most problematic or of greatest concern for you. Picture yourself engaging in behavior representative of this fault.

2. Go to your comfort spot and breathe deeply as you relax your stresses away.

3. Now visualize yourself—with that flaw firmly in mind—as you stand on one side of a bridge that crosses over a rushing stream.

4. Take in your surroundings, greet the water below you and the sky above. Now take a step onto the bridge and begin to cross to the other side.

5. As you cross over, feel yourself become a little more accepting of the flaw you cited. Feel more acceptance with each step. By the time you have crossed to the other side, be aware of a clear sense of acceptance of that particular flaw.

6. Now acknowledge a deep feeling of self-compassion. Forgive yourself for this flaw and all the others that you have. If you'd like, repeat this exercise focusing on the other flaws that you cited. You can also use this exercise as a more general meditation about anything or anyone you wish to leave behind as you cross to a healthier, more joyful state of being. Write out your reactions in your daybook so you can look back at them later.

Like the healing sanctuary we envisioned in chapter three, you can use this crossover visualization exercise any time you feel down on yourself. Accepting yourself, despite your flaws, can help you take action even when you're feeling vulnerable. That is what I mean by "vulnerability is power": Knowing that your flaws, insecurities, and vulnerabilities will not shut you down gives you the power to take the necessary risks to keep moving toward the life you want.

Teresa's story is a perfect, rather excellent, example of this concept. Teresa came to me in the midst of a major life transition. She was desperate to get her career and her family life back on track. Teresa was thirty years old, a single mom, and had been working as a midlevel manager for a large hotel chain based in the northeast. When I started coaching her, Teresa had been fired from her last two jobs and was fearful that her tarnished reputation would prevent her from getting another job, let alone moving up the ladder in an industry she loved.

Though Teresa's professional integrity had never been in question, her lack of experience and judgment had. Compounding that was her status as a single mother, which Teresa felt employers in the fast-paced hotel business held against her. When she first came to see me, Teresa had all but given up on ever finding a job that would allow her to take care of her daughter and herself. She had convinced herself she was worthless and unhireable. Not exactly the qualities you want to put forward as you're beginning an all-out job search.

As we started to unmask Teresa's flaws, real and perceived, she began to see how she had turned every minor mistake into the end of the world. With courage and hard work, Teresa began to view her mistakes as lessons and was able to let go of the harsh judgments she'd held about herself. Once Teresa began to treat herself with the same kind of compassion she'd reserved only for her daughter, she found a level of acceptance about herself and her past actions she never thought possible. With this new outlook, she was able to begin taking steps toward rebuilding her career. After a number of interviews that did not result in job offers, Teresa decided to risk telling the truth about the mistake that had cost her her last job and the fact that she was a single mother. Teresa was overjoyed when her prospective employer, impressed by her honesty and maturity, offered her a great job with an increase in pay. That's the power of acknowledging your faults, feeling your vulnerability and taking the risk anyway.

THE BRIDGE FROM VULNERABILITY TO POWER

Run down your list of faults, then think about what actions you could take to correct or modify each one. Open yourself up to the fact that you might feel fearful just thinking about taking these actions but that you can take them anyway. That's how you change, grow, and Jumpstart Your Life.

Here's a list of my flaws, including what I might do to address each one of them:

1. *I tend to withdraw or hold back.* Don't allow myself to withhold my feelings or fail to express my concerns about a situation. Don't tiptoe around when I'm feeling uncertain in a relationship or work situation; instead, take action. Move forward instead of backward, even if there is no clear-cut, iron-clad right answer. For example, if a friend has done something that has hurt or angered me, I need to let them know my feelings even if I think I might be overreacting.

2. *I let problems reach a boiling point rather than articulating them while they're still manageable.* Speak up before situations become untenable. Work on shortening the amount of time that passes between becoming mindful of an unwanted situation and speaking up about that situation. If my romantic partner or a colleague has upset me, bring it up early as opposed to waiting until it feels hugely insulting or problematic. Don't make mountains out of molehills, but don't ignore the molehills until they become mountains either.

3. *I avoid confrontation.* Take appropriate action when a situation calls for confrontation. Think it through, talk it over with trusted friends or advisors if need be, then speak up.

4. *I overcriticize myself.* Lighten up. Know that I am in control of the volume button on my inner critic and can turn it down or drown it out with positive messages. Do my relaxation and meditation exercises and tools to shift to a more positive state.

5. *I drive myself; I'm sometimes too ambitious.* I accept the fact that I am ambitious and hardworking. Although some people see that as a negative ("you work too hard," "you're never home," etc.), it has helped propel me to a better life for myself and my children. I choose to accept and embrace my driven nature. Again, I can use my relaxation and visualization techniques to chill out once in a while!

Like any other skill, risk-taking is something you build over time. With each success and its subsequent changes, you get stronger and more focused on results. And soon, risk-taking is addictive, a self-perpetuating cycle of taking chances and reaping the rewards. You will fall flat on your face occasionally, which no longer seems so earth-shattering.

SUMMARY: MISTAKE WEDNESDAYS

Teresa was eventually able to see how she had turned every mistake, including the smallest and most insignificant ones, into glaring character disorders and deficiencies of the utmost severity. Once she began to cut herself a little slack and see how hard she'd been on herself, she was able to develop a sense of humor about her over-the-top judgments. Teresa instituted what she called "Mistake Wednesdays," challenging herself to go out and make as many mistakes as she could.

Though it started as a joke for her child's benefit, with Teresa feeding the cat cereal instead of cat food and dropping her daughter off at the supermarket instead of kindergarten, it gave Teresa a refreshing feeling of freedom. Not surprisingly, her daughter caught on to the spirit and soon both of them were making "mistakes" with great abandon.

In this chapter, we looked at self-compassion and self-acceptance. By facing your flaws, you were forced to take a look at how realistic you were in your assessment of your character and where you needed, like Teresa, to lighten up a little. By embracing imperfection, you learned that not every project needs to be tackled on the level of neurosurgery. Sometimes it's better to take a little imperfect action, than none at all.

It feels good to accept myself—flaws, imperfections, vulnerabilities and all—and just be me. Now I find that I am much more accepting of other people as well. I'm more open and less judgmental. In chapter seven, we'll see how my breakthrough experience of breaking off my relationship with Thomas, as well as my stepmother's death, led me to a turning point in my life. Finally, I stopped struggling with all the different aspects of myself, which seemed to be in constant conflict. I began to feel confident enough to take external action based on my newly gained internal clarity. In the next chapter, I'll share some tools like naming and taming your inner voices and inner voice communication, which took my newfound self-acceptance a step further so I could begin to turn my internal turmoil into positive and productive external action.

7

Turning Points

Tuning in to Your Inner Voices

"We're all in this together alone."
—Lily Tomlin

You know those really bad moments in life that would be bad enough all on their own, but in addition to capturing you at your very worst—either as belligerent or reckless or just plain dumb—they also seem to go by in slow motion? Those moments that are like a scene out of an old Peckinpah western with the bullets freezing in midair just before they mow you down, or one of those dreams in which every step feels as if you're fighting your way through a pool of molasses as you flee the bad guys?

I had one of those awful slow-motion moments when I wrecked my brand new BMW. The steel blue BMW which, according to the salesman who'd sold it to me not three weeks before, matched my eyes perfectly. I never even saw it coming, but on a sunny summer afternoon in broad daylight,

I made a left-hand turn into an intersection and sailed right into an oncoming car. While it was happening—in what seemed like slow-motion hours instead of mere seconds—I could see the guy coming toward me in his little red Honda, looking at me through the windshield absolutely aghast. I saw the accident coming, and I saw him seeing me see it coming, but neither of us could do a thing to stop it.

I learned an important lesson about my little blue sedan that day, and that was that in a collision, BMWs are designed to collapse around instead of on their drivers. I didn't get a scratch on me and, fortunately, the man in the Honda wasn't hurt either. My car was another story. My fresh-off-the-line, steel blue BMW that was so new it didn't even have the plates on yet. So new I hadn't figured out how to use the CD player or the in-dash phone. Here was my ultimate driving machine, less than a month old, and already a total wreck. I learned another lesson that day, having nothing to do with European auto design. I learned a lesson about deservedness. And that, for me, was truly a turning point.

As the halfway mark, chapter seven, not coincidentally, is the turning point of this entire book. We're about to weave together all the skills you've learned so far about how to tap in to your internal voice. In this chapter, you'll use that newfound self-awareness as you learn a dynamic method of communication which will allow you integrate the multiple inner messages which you are, by now, beginning to hear loud and clear. With a simple but extremely effective technique I call naming and taming your inner voices, you'll learn to identify and blend the multiple aspects of your personality into one dynamic integrated being who can communicate with nuance, precision, and power. Before we move on to the third step, we'll take that technique even further, into your day-to-day reality, as you master the art of inner voice communication. You'll become adept at making the shift from internal to external as you learn to hear distinct inner voices offering guidance and perspective from different aspects of your personality. You'll learn to identify the voice that would be the most appropriate in a specific situation and to externalize that point of view with that aspect of your personality foremost in your communication. Whether you need to be assertive and direct, gentle and soft-spoken, or open-minded and curious, understanding your inner voices will provide guidance for clear communication.

When I wrecked my new car, my mind was running amok. One voice was consoling, one was chastising, another analyzing. It was like an internal tug of war, pulling me in all directions. Once I sorted out all my voices, I was able to stop being hard on myself for what was, after all, an accident. As I reminded myself to try a little self-compassion, I began to put the collision in perspective. Granted, it would be paperwork and financial repercussions. But no one was hurt, I was fully insured, and the car could be fixed.

So why couldn't I let my consoling, or at least my analytical, side win out over my chastising voice? Why was I so convinced I'd done something unforgivable? Why did I feel I deserved to be punished? As it turned out, I had plenty of time to ponder just that.

When I took my car in to the BMW dealer to have it repaired, there were no replacement parts to be had. I rented a little subcompact, which was all that my insurance would cover. Ever frugal, I refused to spend a dime more than I had to and ended up driving that little car for an entire month before they located the parts we needed. Then, of course, came the actual repair time that was required to get my car running, reconstructed, and repainted. As I drove what was clearly not my brand new steel blue BMW, I listened to all my internal voices, and the loudest ones kept telling me I got what I deserved.

Instead of driving my beautiful new car, the biggest splurge of my entire life, I was right back where I was supposed to be. In that dreary little car with the cigarette burns on the upholstery and the driver side window that wouldn't quite roll up.

But you know what? I rejected that punishing voice. I rejected the notion that I shouldn't have a nice car. I rejected my whole Jane Eyre never quite good enough, always a servant never a guest, recurring life theme. In what was one of my life's turning points, I declared my worthiness. Finally, I had begun to listen to my loving, nourishing voice, which told me I deserved all that life had to offer me. I deserved joy, success, and love. And I certainly deserved my brand new steel blue BMW. In fact, I deserved a whole fleet of BMWs.

INNER VOICES

Whether or not you've ever considered it before today, each of us is a multifaceted being. Think about the different aspects of your personality. Is there a part of you that you think of as the calming presence? A frantic or worrisome piece of you? Maybe a playful, energetic aspect to your personality? Now imagine each facet of your personality as actually having its own voice, articulating that aspect of your personality. That's what I mean by inner voices. Some of these voices may be only internal. Others may be used to communicate externally, which we'll discuss later in this chapter. Each voice represents a distinct part of you. Look at the list of examples of inner voices below to see if any of them fit you.

EXAMPLES OF INNER VOICES

The Leader

The Critic

The Champion

The Long-Suffering Wife

The Worrywart

The Confidante

The Earth Mother

The Follower

The Overspender

The Bitch

The Cheerleader

The Judge

The Servant

The Cheapskate

The Loving Mom

The Provider

The Sexpot

The Strongman

The Clown

The Baby

The Teacher

Imagine a simple "Hi, how are you?" conversation and how different it would sound coming from each of the voices listed above. A greeting from the Sexpot would certainly sound different than one from the Loving Mom, as the Leader's greeting would probably be far different from that of the Servant. In Tool #13, we'll get even more specific as we move on to naming and taming your inner voices.

I've told you much of my personal story from my recurring life themes to my healing imagery. You've already become acquainted with some of those internal voices I experience. Those voices represent facets of my personality, some of which are so different from each other it seems impossible that they could all come from one person. The truth is, you're not one type of person. We are multifaceted beings with a range of thoughts and feelings spanning the entire spectrum of emotions from light to dark. That's why it has always bothered me when someone sums up my personality with just one quality, negating the depth and complexity we all possess.

For example, my mother called me "the picky Virgo." Never mind that I'm a Leo—we didn't get that straightened out until I was in my twenties. Even though the label didn't stick, the sting did. It meant I was snobby and meticulous. In college, I had a professor who, for an entire semester, jokingly called me "the Inquisitor," a reference to my relentless questioning. Well, you already know my theory on flip-side logic. I just turned those baggage tags right over and made them positive instead of negative.

Those were other people's tags for me. I've learned to accept or reject them as I deem appropriate. Sometimes it's a lot more difficult to change our own beliefs about ourselves. Right now, we're dealing with what we—not others—believe about ourselves. Although some healers and educators might disagree with me, I don't think it's a matter of getting rid of the negative aspects of ourselves, because I'm not convinced that doing so is possible, or even healthy. Rather than reject the negative aspects of ourselves, what we tend to think of as our dark sides, I believe we should acknowledge, embrace, and even nurture those less desirable parts of our being.

For example, when I crashed my BMW, the negative or dark side of me came out loud and strong about my inherent unworthiness. I crashed the car, that voice told me, because

I just plain didn't deserve something that nice. My old belief, caused by all the little slights as well as the big traumas of my life, had become a wound which was linked to my dark side and manifested in that persistent negative voice. Although that feeling of unworthiness may never go away completely, I can now attribute it to one aspect of myself rather than give that negativity free rein over my entire being. Even though that dark side is still present, it's now manageable. I control it instead of letting it control me. That's an example of naming and taming our inner voices.

Rather than ignore or live in denial about our old wounds, I think we should see them for what they are, recognizing how far we've come in our healing process. These wounds don't go away, they just scab and then scar over, and they can open up if they're picked or prodded. We need to know where they are and what might open them up, in order to protect those vulnerable spots as we move along our healing path. That's why it's so important to be familiar with our various internal voices, so we can keep the negative inner voices in check and bring the positive voices forward when we need them.

I've identified a number of inner voices that are representative of the lighter and darker sides of my personality. When I hear their voices in my head or see them in writing my verbal meditations, they each have a distinctive rhythm and language. Some are strong and direct, others are more gentle. As I've refined them over the years, I've witnessed how useful these inner voices can be in managing different types of situations in my life.

First, there's the CEO, my very adult and in-charge businesswoman. She is thoughtful and professional, always prepared and articulate, occasionally a little too overbearing and driven. The Ever-Striving Mom is the voice of the parent that I try to be: loving and giving of my time and energy, but always with an undercurrent of unease that I'm not doing all that I can do as a parent. Then there's the Saloon Girl, the rebellious part of me that can be quite useful in cutting through red tape and corporate nonsense. She's feisty, full of attitude, and never afraid to say what's on her mind. The Producer speaks for my creative side. I tend to think of that voice in male terms: He's smart, strong, creative, and always in control. Balancing out these disparate voices is the Diplomat. Borne of my chaotic childhood, the Diplomat strives for peace and resolution and is often a calming voice in times of crisis or dischord.

Tool # 13: Naming and Taming Your Inner Voices

After participating in one of my workshops on naming and taming your inner voices, a police detective came up to me in tears, profoundly affected by the exercise I'm about to share with you. She told me that as a female officer she knew she had to approach her job differently from the men with whom she worked. She understood full well that, at different times, she was expected to be supercop, mother confessor, babysitter, one of the boys, and shrink. But until that day, she had never understood that what she was doing instinctively could be done consciously, that she could refine each one of these distinct roles, recognize which would be most effective in a given situation, and tune in to the voice that would give her the guidance she needed in the moment. When her male partner needed an on-the-job collaborator, she was all supercop, but when he was looking for a sympathetic ear to discuss a personal problem, she could soften into the more appropriate role of mother confessor or lay therapist. When this concept came into focus for her, she discovered she had a powerful framework for thinking about and articulating different aspects of her personality as the occasion dictated.

As you'll see, this method is applicable to your interactions with other people—at home, at work, or socially. The technique gives you the language and skills to help you communicate at an optimum level with your clients, colleagues, children, spouse, and friends. I'll give you an example. Two TV producers to whom I'd taught this technique were trying to coach a relatively inexperienced actress for a series of television commercials. In attempting to be "a TV personality," the actress had lost the girl-from-Nebraska quality that had landed her the job in the first place. As the producers helped her get back in touch with her "midwestern girl" voice, she nailed the approachable essence they were looking for and sailed successfully through the production.

Are you beginning to sense how useful this tool can be in your everyday life? I've had people tell me the naming and taming your inner voices exercise has given them confidence, clarity, and the ability to communicate more powerfully and effectively than ever before. It's not all that difficult to master, as you're about to see. Here's what I want you to do. Read through the following description a couple of times, then go to the place that you've already designated as the spot where you can relax and meditate comfortably, without interruption. Don't worry that you'll forget the specifics of the exercise; if you have the big picture, you'll be fine. Alternatively, if you want someone to read the exercise for you, enlist a trusted friend or partner and have them slowly and gently guide you through this meditation as you relax and focus.

Let's get started:

1. Close your eyes, relax, and concentrate on your breathing to get into a deep meditative state. Release any tension you've been holding onto, focusing on different parts of your body as you let go of stress.

2. Picture a dinner table—which could be anything from a giant banquet table to a humble kitchen table—around which your dinner party guests will be seated.

3. Now look around your table and imagine all the different aspects of yourself sitting there. They might be warm and friendly toward each other, standoffish and distant, or even combative. Allow yourself to create an image or character for each of those aspects. Get a clear sense of each one's demeanor, gender, age, and style.

4. Go around the table, from one character to the next. You may have as few as three or four or as many as a dozen. Now, allow yourself to give each character a voice as they introduce themselves by name. For example, "I'm the Judge," "I'm the Long-Suffering Wife," or "I'm the CEO."

5. After you've let your dinner party unfold, taking note of the dialogue and relationships among your inner voices, it's time to bring your gathering to a close. Pick a unifying gesture—a song, a cheer, a toast, or a prayer—to conclude your dinner party and bring a sense of completion and unity to this meditation.

6. After you've finished your closing ritual, open your eyes and come back to real-world focus. Immediately record the names and descriptions of your inner voice characters in your Traveling Hopefully Daybook, as well as any remarks about each one.

How was that experience for you? Were there any surprises? Was there a leader among your group? Who was hesitant to enter into the conversation? Who was talkative? Was anyone argumentative? Were your voices at war? At peace? Can you begin to get a sense of how and when you would call upon a particular aspect of yourself, using that voice to aid you in your communication? Either to give you encouragement when you need it or to remind you to forgive yourself for mistakes?

SHIFTING FROM INTERNAL TO EXTERNAL

I originally created the exercise above as a way to understand and rationalize all my conflicting feelings about myself, my work, and my relationships. Back then, I thought most of my problems had to do with my career. If I could just climb up to the next rung on the corporate ladder, everything would be fine. So I used naming and taming your inner voices, as well as the following exercise, to help me communicate more effectively on the job with colleagues, both subordinates and superiors. Only later—after I'd had my midlife epiphany and decided that I would do what was necessary to ensure that the second half of my life would be much more joyful than the first half—did I begin to use this technique in my personal life as well. That's when I began to look at my negative recurring themes to see how my management of my inner voices was either helping or hurting my growth. As the positive voices that brought comfort and inspiration into my life began to grow stronger, and the darker, negative aspects receded further into the background, I began to examine my external actions, starting with my career.

After heading up corporate communications and media relations departments at three major entertainment companies, I'd finally admitted to myself that I'd worked really hard to get exactly where I didn't want to be. I began to form a plan, which was the genesis of the Fourth Step to Jumpstart Your

Life—creating a Traveling Hopefully Personal Road map— which we'll discuss in a later chapter. I had reached a cross- road, a turning point brought on by my burning desire to change. That's when I began to figure out how to tune into and manage my inner voices so that they could help me speak out, transforming my life, first professionally and later personally.

Since I firmly believe that chaos breeds opportunity in the workplace, I waited until the moment was right, when my company was going through a major corporate transition, to make my move. After turning down yet another senior com- munications position, which would have taken me even fur- ther down the path I didn't wish to travel, but which most people seemed to think was a great move, I pitched for a "cre- ative job" developing reality shows. That may not seem like a badge of honor to a lot of people, especially now that reality TV's been done to death. But the freedom and fun involved in developing television shows instead of promoting them after someone else has created them was a huge turning point for me. To the surprise of many people around me, although not to my inner guides who were just waiting for me to get my creative act together, I was actually good at my new TV job, taking creative ideas and developing them from concept through production. Finally, I was doing it—I was success- fully working my way down the corporate ladder—toward a life that suited me, all of me, much better than the one I'd been living. I lost my Senior V. P. stripes, my staff, and a ton of management headaches in the process. Instead, I found the courage to come out the shadows and start traveling hope- fully, one baby step at a time.

A couple of baby steps forward often meant a big step backward. Even though I was beginning to change inter- nally, that didn't mean those changes were manifesting exter- nally. This period of baby-stepping into the changes I had envisioned was precisely when I wrecked my BMW (did I mention that it was steel blue?) and had to begin the arduous task of naming and taming my inner voices all over again. As I went back to all the tools that I've shared with you in this book, retreating to my healing sanctuary, having long conversations with my future self, and posing powerful questions every night in my Traveling Hopefully Daybook, I finally understood the message—the negative life theme—I'd been feeding myself about how I was undeserving and unloveable and how that had resulted in a devastating lack of confidence and self-esteem. That's when my internal voice of compassion drowned out all the others—and I crossed over to an inner feeling of worthiness.

Gradually, the people around me began to see evidence of my transformation. I had changed jobs, bought and wrecked a new car, lost twenty-five pounds, and grown my neat working mom hair long for the first time in years. I gave all my buttoned-down corporate suits to a women's shelter and bought all new clothes that reflected my newfound style. Bold, fun, sexy. Eventually, after some fashions don'ts that made me feel like a lounge singer wannabe, I learned to manage which of my inner voices got to vote on my wardrobe. I found a hip but slightly more conservative look that fit the new me. I was successfully learning to integrate all aspects of my personality, and it was, undoubtedly, beginning to pay off. Whether the outside world applauded or threw tomatoes made little difference—I was willing to be noticed.

Just because I finally began to feel worthy didn't mean anyone else had noticed anything new, except my size four leather pants, that is. There might have been a little less of me, but other than that, I was exactly who I'd always been before—the hardworking, never too demanding, always there to serve employee. Only now I had a few secret weapons to call upon, namely my inner voices. When I felt I needed a little righteous indignation because I'd been slighted on the job or just needed a dash of feistiness to pull off a risky idea, I'd unleash the rebellious Saloon Girl. Or when the stakes were high on a creative project, I'd bring out the Producer who had the guts and pizzazz to throw any idea on the table, undaunted by potential criticism. And, of course, the CEO was always right there, diplomatically managing and balancing it all like a true professional. Don't get me wrong. I wasn't playacting a role. This was all me, just guided by the inner voices to have the confidence and communication skills I needed to suit the scenario.

Since I was now finding myself in unfamiliar situations and meeting new people regularly—the creative, high-power types whom I would have found intimidating just a little while before—I needed to find a way to navigate these uncharted waters. I took my system of internal communication outward. Now that I'd harnessed my inner voices and learned to bring them out when I needed them, it was time to try a little role-playing with the inner voices of the significant people in my life. Let me explain what I mean.

You know that moment when your boss walks in the door and, just from her "Good morning" or "Any calls?" you can tell what kind of mood she's in? You know immediately if she's the "Boss from Hell" or the "Magnanimous Mentor." You've already summed her up her mood, nonverbal behavior, and tone of voice, and can probably imagine the inner voices that are talking in her head. Some people call this intuitive process "reading the room," and it's a survival instinct that can help you enormously in your personal and professional lives. If you're not sure that you possess those skills— or maybe you're not even sure what I'm talking about—don't worry. You're about to develop them. If you've already got great people instincts, we'll be taking them to an entirely new level as we learn a process of inner voice role-playing a key conversation with the outcome you desire, between you and a significant person. From there, it's only one more step to have that conversation in the real world. Hold on, as we make that shift from internal to external through inner voice communication.

Tool # 14: Inner Voice Communication

Just because I was starting to feel the effects of my transformation, doesn't mean the people in my life necessarily transformed along with me. I had work to do, and that's when my internal communication went external. I developed a way of thinking about how my inner voices would communicate with other people's inner voices, then how that process might take place in the real world. It's what I sometimes call "writing the script and waiting for the moment." It allowed me to role-play different conversations, discussions, even professional presentations, before taking them to the external level. Sometimes it was uncanny how closely a real conversation mirrored the inner voice one I'd just had in my head.

IDENTIFYING THREE KEY INNER VOICES OF A SIGNIFICANT PERSON IN YOUR LIFE

In a moment, I'm going to ask you to choose a key person in your life, then identify three voices which represent different aspects of his or her personality. You can consider those aspects of the other person in isolation or in relation to you, or both, whatever is more useful. I've looked at a number of colleagues in this way and also think about my children's key voices. Whether you do this exercise with or without the person's awareness is up to you. If you choose to clue him in as to how you characterize his voices, make sure you choose your appropriate voice to do the job so you'll be received as communicative and not manipulative. You'll see what I mean by that when you read number two below.

Here's what I want you to do:

1. Identify a significant person in your life with whom you regularly interact. Pick someone with whom you'd like to improve communication or deepen the relationship. This can be someone you're involved with romantically, professionally, or as a friend or family member.

2. Next, think of three distinct aspects of his or her personality that you are aware of. Ideally, these should be aspects of this person with which you are familiar and can think of in terms of having distinct voices. If you need some help, look back at our list of examples of inner voices.

3. Now, just as you named your inner voices, give this person's three key voices names or titles that exemplify those particular aspects of the person.

Since I just told you about my switch from corporate to creative professional, I'll use the example of Lonnie, my new boss in my development job.

Here's how I thought of three key inner voices I heard from Lonnie:

1. Big Brother. Lonnie was one of the best bosses I ever had. He is very comfortable being in charge, and at times I could clearly hear a sort of protectiveness, almost like a big brother.

2. Creative Partner. Lonnie has great creative instincts and also enjoys collaboration, both welcome traits in a creative executive and a boss. But he'd had to overcome an unjustified industry perception that if you didn't come up through the creative ranks or from another industry where you held a creative position, you weren't creative. Hooey.

3. Tough Guy. The flip-side to the Big Brother, Lonnie's Tough Guy could be very protective but also a little dangerous. A pissed-off idealist, the Tough Guy came on strong, but instead of wanting to talk things through, he'd rather break your kneecaps.

IMAGINE A CRITICAL CONVERSATION BETWEEN YOUR INNER VOICE AND THAT OF YOUR SIGNIFICANT PERSON

Now that you've identified three key personality voices in your significant person, we're going to look at a critical conversation between your inner voice and theirs. This is a great way to determine the content, tone, and timing of important discussions like asking your boss for a raise or dealing with delicate relationship or parenting issues. By choosing your appropriate inner voice, as well as identifying which voice you want to tap into in your significant person, you improve the chance for a quality dialogue with an outcome you've already determined and rehearsed. Your conversation won't always go the way you've envisioned it, of course, but you'll greatly increase your odds for success.

Going back to my relationship with Lonnie, let's imagine a scenario where this concept could be effective. Say, for example, that I wanted to convince Lonnie that I was the right person to oversee a creative project that was extremely challenging because of the high costs and difficult personalities involved. Using inner voice communication, here's what I would do:

- Identify the inner voice that could most effectively have that conversation with Lonnie. I pick the Producer, who has the leadership skills as well as the business and creative savvy to pull off the job.
- Determine to which of Lonnie's key voices to appeal. I pick the Creative Partner because this project definitely calls for collaboration.
- In my mind, I create the scenario of my Producer talking to Lonnie's Creative Partner. I state my desire to handle the project and offer compelling arguments to support my request.
- I envision Lonnie's Creative Partner reacting to me, knowing from past experience the types of arguments and objections he might raise. In my mind, I deflect these and further support my case.
- Finally, when I feel that the real-world moment is right and that Lonnie is receptive—that it, that my Producer can effectively appeal to his Creative Partner—I open the discussion in the external world.

As Stephen Covey says, "Begin with the end in mind." In these key conversations, you will have already determined your desired outcome and the arguments you'll use to support it. By rehearsing the discussion in your head, your inner voice speaking to your significant person's inner voice, you can try out tactics and role-play objections without risking the real conversation. That's how inner voice communication builds clarity and confidence.

Here's a recap of the process. Now you give it a try:

- Identify a critical conversation you'd like to have with a significant person in your life.

- Determine your best inner voice for that discussion.
- Identify the appropriate inner voice to which you plan to appeal in your significant person. In other words, are you asking your Needy Child to approach your Bean Counter Boss for a raise? You might want to re-consider that match, and have your Rising Star speak to his Nurturing Manager.
- Imagine this key conversation. Add a few challenging twists and turns, so you can be as prepared as possible for the real conversation.
- Now take your internal conversation external. When you sense that your significant person is most recep-tive, open your discussion with the inner voice you've chosen to represent you in this particular scenario. Find the tone that will most likely evoke the inner voice of theirs that you've predetermined is the best fit for this conversation.

Maybe you're one of those rare people who finds the right tone, the right arguments, and the right moment every time you have a critical conversation in either your personal or professional life. Perhaps you even enlist a trusted advi-sor to coach you before you try out the real thing, as I fre-quently do with my clients. I applaud your foresight and preparation.

Most of us, however, just plunge into career negotiations, relationship discussions, and other key conversations with barely a second thought, let alone attempting the strategic approach I'm suggesting here. But what do you have to lose by trying out a discussion internally before risking it exter-nally? Not a thing, and you've possibly quite a bit to gain.

Let's look at some of your inner voices and how they might—or might not—match up with the significant people in your life when having those critical conversations. See if any of your scenarios and inner voice match-ups are similar.

INNER VOICE MATCH-UPS

YOUR VOICE	THEIR VOICE	MATCH?
The Leader	The Follower	YES
The Critic	The Judge	NO
The Champion	The Servant	YES
The Bean Counter	The Overspender	NO
The Bitch	The Cheerleader	NO
The Teacher	The Confidante	YES
The Loving Mom	The Baby	YES
The Sexpot	The Worrywart	NO

As they say in the car commercials, your results may vary. Obviously, these are generalizations to get you thinking about how different personality aspects might logically match up to each other. Relationships are multilayered and unpredictable, of course, and opposites do occasionally not only attract but complement one another, so only you can judge the dynamics of your particular situation. Take your list of inner voices from the naming and taming exercise and line it up against the list of inner voices you identified from the significant person in your life to see how you think you might match up.

This will give you a way of thinking about intercommunication so you can have your script ready and wait for the right moment. If you're one of those people who always seems to get the tone or the timing of a key conversation wrong, this framework will be especially effective in helping you improve your communications. Like athletes who envision the golf stroke or the touchdown in their minds before they see it on the green or the field, inner preparation is half the game.

It all goes back to instinct and timing. Rather than waiting to guess how to interact with your boss, friend, spouse, or kids most effectively, you'll now have a process from which to initiate the interaction. Rest assured that this is not intended to minimize or oversimplify the complexity of human nature. In fact, it's exactly the opposite. It's meant to help organize your thoughts and give you a constructive way to approach that complexity.

SUMMARY: FLUFFY BABY KITTEN GOES ON A DATE

If you think the "Fluffy Baby Kitten" reference in the title above means I'm about to tell you a Dick and Jane–style children's story, guess again. Fluffy Baby Kitten was actually a label I was given at a business conference.

When I recently attended a three-day training workshop, one of the exercises required that we identify and label a characteristic in each participant that seemed to be underutilized or shoved into the background of that person's communication style. As you might imagine, it was an extraordinary experience to have a group of people you've only known for a couple of days sum up what they consider to be your most overlooked asset. This group had a pretty good read on me — they saw that I was cerebral, hardworking, and dynamic. They also saw that I was afraid of having other people take care of me or of letting the more vulnerable aspects of my personality come into a professional scenario for fear of appearing weak. The image they decided should be my reminder to tap into that vulnerable self was "a fluffy baby kitten that just wanted to be petted and fed." It's amazing how clearly people sometimes see us, even when we're convinced that we're able to hide certain aspects of ourselves.

I've never forgotten that very fitting and slightly comical

image of the little furry kitty; in fact, it's often the image I use when I'm in social situations like (gulp) first dates. That's not really the time I need to be the hard-headed businesswoman or the complicated artist. I just need to be a girl—vulnerable, warm, and open to being taken care of on occasion by someone else.

As you can see, there are all sorts of ways to employ the tools I've shared with you in chapter seven, naming and taming your inner voices and inner voice communication, both at work and at home. Sizing up a situation in advance, including giving some thought about which of your inner voices is best to guide you in a specific scenario, can greatly reduce your stress as it increases your effectiveness.

In the next chapter we'll roll on with momentum, forging ahead as we tackle the beginning stages of creating a Traveling Hopefully Personal Road map by distinguishing goals from dreams. Unlike vague plans, which look toward the future but fail to hold you accountable for it, your road map will be a custom blueprint for change. We'll actually be jumping ahead to the Fourth Step to Jumpstart Your Life, which we'll finalize when we bring your road map to life in a later chapter. For now, let's keep building your foundation for positive life change.

8

Momentum

Goal-Setting and Downhill Gliding

"Wanna fly, you got to give up the
shit that weighs you down."

—Toni Morrison

Remember the kid's board game Chutes and Ladders? It had one hundred little squares on the board and the object was to be the first one to the top. While you were working your way up to the final blue ribbon square, if you did something really good like rescuing a stranded kitty from a tree, you got to take a shortcut and zoom right up the ladder. But if you did something really bad like smashing a baseball through a window, you had to slide down a chute and start the arduous climb all over again. So how did you make sure you climbed the ladder and avoided the chute? In the game, of course, it's all about chance landings. The sheer unpredictably is what makes it fun. But what about in real life? Now that you've done the difficult inner homework to determine what's going to bring more passion and purpose into your life, how do you take matters in your own hands, avoid the chance backsliding, and put your action plan on the fast track so that your climb up the ladder is swift? How do you create the kind of momentum that will keep you traveling hopefully at a steady clip instead of falling down the inevitable chutes that life places in your path?

In this chapter we'll take a jump ahead to begin to explore the foundation of the Fourth Step to Jumpstart Your Life, which is to create a Traveling Hopefully Personal Road map. In a later chapter, we'll put all the pieces you've been learning about together to design your road map as a written blueprint for the life you want. To get us started, we're going to do some basic goal-setting, as well as building a timetable which will help you set realistic priorities. As you work your way through this chapter, remember that we're not attempting to transform your entire life overnight. If you bite off too much, you risk getting overwhelmed and shutting down altogether. Don't let yourself off the hook by neglecting to map out some baby steps that will get you closer to your goals. As those baby steps start to add up, you'll be on your way.

At this point in our personal journey, some of the steps will overlap or seem to be out of sequence. Don't worry, it's all part of the process as you learn the basics then add new depth and layers to your foundation for change. We'll also begin to pick up speed so it's important to understand the concept of momentum. Although some might consider momentum an abstract notion, you know me well enough by now to know that I am nothing if not practical. We're not looking at momentum as an idea, we're looking at it as an integral part of your master plan, the jet fuel behind your personal road map for defining, refining, and jumpstarting your best possible life. I don't want it to take you forty years, as it did me, to figure out that you deserve to be happy and that you can design a rich, fulfilling life based on your unique gifts. Let's take that big-picture vision you've been formulating throughout the past seven chapters and focus it down to its most aerodynamic form as you define your goals, build a timetable, and let momentum take over!

POSITIONING YOURSELF FOR SUCCESS

Sometimes you've got to look all the way down the road in order to see which path you should take to get you where you want to go. Even if you know where you're headed, it's easy to get sidetracked. If you start off with no idea where you're going, you are definitely setting yourself up for a lifetime of detours. That process of looking at the end goal or big picture, and then breaking it down into bottom-line action steps will help you position yourself for success and become the foundation of your personal road map. That requires that you begin to set goals, determine priorities, and establish a time frame, which the tools in this chapter will help you to do.

If you're one of those people who thinks goal-setting is an exercise in futility, because you're simply setting yourself up to lose by falling short of your desired outcome, maybe it's time to change your perspective by employing a little flip-side logic. Look at it this way: If you set a goal to record a CD of your original music within the next six months and you only complete ten of the twelve songs you intend to include — are you a winner or a loser? Incredible as it seems, many people consider themselves failures when they fall even a little short of a predetermined goal. Not me. If I had ten songs out of the twelve, I'd consider that a monumental success. Keep in mind, I'm not talking about things that you are contractually or morally obligated to complete within a certain timetable or standard of quality. As soon as I finished my happy dance over my ten new songs, I'd regroup and set a new goal of finishing the last two within a newly determined time frame. Again, it's all in your perspective and how you choose to define success.

Of course, you need to set realistic goals in the first place, and you need to understand that it's up to you to adjust them as you go. As in all the other exercises you've done so far, you are in control and thus free to change your mind and make course corrections as you travel. Setting realistic goals within a reasonable time frame and then prioritizing them according to which are most important to you is a critical aspect of traveling hopefully. Only when you know where to put your energy can you start taking meaningful action.

On the other hand, sometimes even taking the wrong action is better than taking no action at all. The momentum involved in actively following your plan for success will enable you to make the necessary adjustments more easily. Remember in chapter five when I described how I had shifted my torturous self-image as the sweaty rock climber, always striving for the summit to the infinitely more liberating downhill glider? That change of perspective helped me see that if I stayed in motion, picking up speed as I coasted downhill, it was easy to shift directions. Even if you realize you're heading down the wrong path, it's not difficult to correct your course if you're already moving. As we learned in high school science class, if you're inert—not moving at all—it's much harder to get started, let alone build the momentum needed to make that directional change.

You might be one of the lucky ones who has so many goals that you just don't know where to start. That's my definition of a high-class problem, a sort of embarrassment of riches. You have so much drive, energy, and passion and so many ideas that you're simply at a loss as to where to begin. Some people actually shut down when they're overcome by too many options. Well, we certainly don't want all that healthy ambition to go to waste.

Whether you're goal-phobic or overwhelmed by a bounty of choices, let's start positioning you for success by looking at what success means to you. Remember when you met your future self in chapter three? It's time to catch up with that image of yourself again, so let's get a little momentum going as we take a big leap forward—all the way to your one-hundredth birthday.

YOUR HUNDREDTH BIRTHDAY PARTY

I want you to imagine this scenario. You've just turned one hundred years old, and all your friends and family have gathered together to celebrate the momentous occasion. You're feeling great, looking great, and all your faculties are intact. As you listen to the adults describing you and your life to your grandchildren and great grandchildren, what do you hear them saying? What do they tell the kids that you did with your life? With your one hundred years on the planet?

Step back and reflect on what you imagine others will say about your life when it is nearly over. Really think about what you want your life to amount to as you listen in on that birthday party for a moment. What kinds of things get mentioned? What are you the most proud of? What do you think is missing from the comments people are making at your final birthday bash? What do you want to make sure gets said about you? What would you feel you'd missed out on if it weren't listed as part of your legacy?

Now is the time to figure out how you want your life to be described—while you still have the time to create it. Determining your goals, picking priorities, and setting a timetable will help you in that very crucial process as you create your personal road map. Then, as you streamline and focus that vision, momentum can take over.

GOALS: DREAMS WITH DEADLINES

After I articulated my dream of making the second half of my life more joyful than the first half, I saw that I had some hard work ahead of me in defining exactly what that meant. Unsure where to begin the daunting process of reinventing my life, I kept coming back to what I understood best — business — and began to think of myself as my own client. I felt a little sheepish about carrying on this dialogue with myself about myself, but plunged ahead nonetheless. I asked myself: If I came to me as a client seeking expertise in creating and communicating an image for my business or product, where would I start? And then, feeling more foolish by the minute, I answered myself: I'd start with the basics of setting goals that were a reflection of who I was, what I wanted, and how I was going to get it.

I'd always loved the old saying "Goals are dreams with deadlines," because it took a fuzzy sort of vision and translated it into action. That became my personal credo as I launched into planning mode. I was having a great time in my television development job, helping to get interesting and talented folks like psychic medium John Edward on the air. Now that the floodgates of my own creativity had cracked open a bit, I was finding that it just wasn't enough for me. Although I was evolving professionally, I was still living the old Jane Eyre overworked and underacknowledged theme, assisting others in living their dreams instead of going after my own. At about this time, painful personal challenges joined complex professional ones, and both my father's health and the solidity of my marriage began to weaken.

I was flying back and forth to the east coast every month to oversee production on a talk show that was taped in New York and had a lot of time in the air to think about where I was headed, metaphorically speaking, that is. I began to formulate a list of goals, which included leaving the corporate world, writing, producing, and teaching. I had no idea how I would accomplish any of this, I just knew they were on the list and that I wanted to accomplish them all within the next five years. Once I had a list of goals and a timetable, I instinctively started to make those items priorities in my life. Initially, I experimented my way through that process; now I have a much more systematic approach to setting goals and deadlines.

Not surprisingly given my own background, I had always been fascinated by the way people structured their families and interacted, or failed to do so, as a group. Since my husband and I had been living a role-reversal of the traditional marriage and parenting structuring with him at home and me at work, I was interested in how other stay-at-home dad/working mom families divvied up responsibilities in their home, in terms of parenting tasks, money, and chores. I wondered what shortcuts I could learn from them, how successful their marriages were, and how their children were turning out. Since I could find very little information on the subject, I decided to investigate the topic myself, talking to parents and learning as much as I could.

I am convinced that I would never have turned the results of my investigation into a book had writing not been an item on my list of professional goals. I would merely have set off on an exploratory journey, met a lot of great parents along the way, and satisfied my curiosity. Somewhere the idea that this was information to be shared—and that I was capable of writing it and having it published—grew into action. It was almost as though, having found a place on my written list, my goal took on a life of its own despite any trepidation or hesitation I might have had. With that first bit of success—having a book published—I began to feel stronger, more willing to embrace imperfection, and take the necessary risks that would allow me to change my life. Suddenly, I was in charge.

Tool # 15: Discovering the Power of the 3 P's

Right now, we're going to begin to focus on goals. So get out your Traveling Hopefully Daybook or a notepad and get ready to write. Take three sheets of paper, or three pages in your daybook, and label each page with one of the following headings: PROFESSIONAL, PERSONAL, and POSSESSIONS. In a moment, I'm going to ask you to list your goals in each of these three distinct areas.

Like all the other exercises we've done, this is not about how well you write or how clever you can be. It's about honesty and the willingness to dig deep. Don't censor yourself or worry that your categories might overlap. You can shift things around later. Don't be concerned about priorities or timing. We're casting a wide net which we'll narrow down later, so list anything that crosses your mind. For now, get your wish list for life down on paper.

1. PROFESSIONAL

In the first column—PROFESSIONAL—list everything you want to accomplish in your job or career. And if you've already accomplished a lot, list the goals that will bring you to the next level—or if you've been yearning to make a career change, come up with goals in a completely new area. Remember, this is blue sky time. List everything you've ever passionately dreamed about or considered in passing. And if you don't have or don't want a career, just list everything that falls more into the business side of life than the personal. Because everyone has money to manage and a household to run. Include business goals you have, college degrees you want, awards you'd like to win, how much money you want to make, but not how you'd like to spend it. We'll get to that in the third column.

Your professional goals might include some of the following:

- Get a new job.
- Take courses or get an advanced degree.
- Start your own business.
- Secure a promotion.
- Achieve a career milestone like an award or professional accomplishment.
- Hit a financial target.

2. PERSONAL

In this column include all your relationship, spiritual, and personal growth goals. Do you want to get married? Have a family? Have more or better friendships? Do you want to learn another language? Get on an exercise program? Find a church or temple? Do you want to start singing? Write a book? Learn to play tennis or guitar?

Don't worry if some of these seem to overlap with professional goals; you can refine things later. Right now, just let your ideas flow.

Consider these personal goals and then add more of your own:

- Find a romantic relationship.
- Improve the relationship you're in.

- Enhance your parenting skills.
- Learn to dance.
- Identify a church, temple, or place of worship.
- Pursue a hobby like gardening, chess, or playing the piano.
- Join a club or organization.
- Get involved in politics or charitable cause.
- Find a creative outlet like painting or singing.
- Get on a fitness regimen.
- Have more fun and adventure.
- Learn a language.
- Build new friendships.
- Lose weight.
- Master a sport.
- Spend more time in nature.

3. POSSESSIONS

In the third column, list all the material things you want to have around you and those you love. I should warn you, this is the category that people usually find the most difficult. Many of us have been brought up to believe that it's bad to be materialistic, it's wrong to want nice things, or that we're shallow if we care about possessions. Nonsense. I think it's very wrong to value things above people, but what's the harm in preferring nice things to not nice things? Seems like a no-brainer to me.

Even if it's difficult for you to shake up your abundance-is-bad mentality, let's just pretend for now that you've put your limiting prejudices aside. Here's your chance to list all the things you'd like to have. And don't forget, this stuff is for other's people's benefit, too, not just your own. Feel better now?

Write down all the things you'd like to own: a nice house, an art collection, some great playground equipment for the kids, a convertible, a brand-new wardrobe. Whatever it is, put it on your POSSESSIONS list. Again, don't worry about how important each item is to you. We'll get to all that when we rank our priorities by creating a timetable. At that point, some of these things will undoubtedly come off your list. Have some fun—there's that word again—and I promise I won't tell anyone that you're secretly craving a little boy's vintage Rolex watch. Oh wait, that's me!

My 3 P's list looked like this:

PROFESSIONAL

Continue to build my business

Hire great people

Increase my earnings

Buy apartment/condo building

Write a new nonfiction book

Write a syndicated self-help column

Build speaking business

Have a radio show

Write a novel

Assist others in creating nontraditional businesses

Create secondary business

PERSONAL

Spend lots of time with my kids

Find a husband and get married again

Get personal trainer and get in shape

Take salsa or ballroom dance lessons

Take kids to Europe

Go to the Amazon

Find a spiritual community that's a good fit for me

Make home improvements

Convert garage to guest house

Re-landscape

Learn to play tennis

Get scuba certified

Lose ten pounds

Research retirement locations

POSSESSIONS

Diamond ring (to go with husband)

Pickup truck for my gardening stuff

Collection of original California art

Some first editions

A real CD collection

A real CD player instead of the junk I have

Good computer system

"Media room" for kids

"Teenager" furniture for kids' rooms

New wardrobe (for newly trained figure)

Retirement property/house

Okay, I admit it, the boy's vintage Rolex watch

Whew! Looking at my 3 P's list almost wore me out. It's a good thing we're about to get to the prioritizing, because I know I can't bite off all of this at once. Truthfully, I find it energizing and inspiring to look down my list of goals. Just by identifying what my goals are, I'm already closer to the life I want. I am confident that when I look back, in a year or a decade, that I will have accomplished a lot of things on my list.

Were you surprised by any of the things on your 3 P's list? Most of them have probably been percolating for a while now, right? What we're going to do—starting now and all the way to the end of the book—is to systematically build your prioritized goals into a detailed Traveling Hopefully Personal Road map, complete with action steps and accountability. The road map will also include your plan for a support system and fallback position so that when setbacks and disappointments occur—and they inevitably will—you'll be prepared.

It would be nice if we could successfully overhaul every sector of our life today before lunch, but creating unrealistic timelines will position us for failure. In order to get a sense of when you would like to reach all of the goals on your 3 P's list, I invite you to take the timeline test.

Tool # 16: Putting Your Goals to the Timeline Test

Back to my favorite old expression, "Goals are dreams with deadlines." It's great to have a goal, but are you willing to attach a date to it? Is it a distant dream or something that you have a burning desire to make happen in the very near future? Putting your goals to the timeline test is a pretty strong indicator of how anxious you are to realize them.

Remember when we talked about embracing imperfection in chapter six? Before we go any further with creating your timetable, I want to take that concept to its next level and talk about embracing failure. Don't worry—it's not nearly as negative as it sounds. In fact, once you adjust your definition of failure, it's downright liberating. Many people refuse to set goals because they feel that once they articulate one, they've set themselves up to fail unless they succeed one hundred percent. Just as we learned to rethink perfection, let's just change our definition of failure. Simple as that. To me, failure only occurs when you fail to learn. If I screw something up mightily and don't learn the lesson the first time, guess what happens? I usually screw it up again and then I learn my lessons and move on to bungling bigger and better things. It's just as you tell your kids or were told when you were a kid: If you learn something, anything, from your so-called failures, then they're not failures. They're valuable lessons propelling you toward your goals.

Some people define goals as activities or outcomes that are within your control. In other words, you can set a goal of recording your CD of original music, but you can't necessarily set a goal that you will sell that CD, get signed by a label and become an international rock star, because you don't control that outcome. I define goals as what you want to achieve, attain, or accomplish in your life—all those items we listed in the 3 P's exercise—knowing that you may not control the big-picture outcome or end result, because you don't run the universe, but you do control the bottom-line action steps of each goal. That's why we'll be breaking down your big-picture goals into those specific bottom-line action steps in a later chapter. Right now, we're going to look at how time-sensitive each of your goals is to you.

Now that you've adjusted your definition of failure, taking a significant amount of pressure off yourself in the process, let's put your goals to the timeline test by seeing where each one stacks up on the priority scale. Here's what I want you to do:

1. Take a look at your 3 P's list. Starting first with your list of professional goals, put a number beside each item indicating within what year time frame you want to accomplish it. In other words, if you listed "start my own business," is that something that you want to make happen within a year or five years? Knowing when you want to reach a particular goal will tell you how important and immediate it really is to you. For the sake of simplicity it's easiest to break down the timeline by limiting yourself to one, three, five, ten or L, which stands for sometime within your lifetime. These numbers—and the letter L—signify when you want to reach each goal. If you're dead set on listing the target year, month, day, and hour next to each goal, knock yourself out and be as specific as you like.

2. Next go to your personal list and do the same thing. Although it may be contradictory to your thinking, you can even set a time frame within which you want to get married. Do you want to find a spouse and marry within one year, three years, five years, ten years or just sometime within your lifetime? Wanting to find an appropriate life partner and get married within a year (my goal) sets up a different level of urgency and action than just generally wanting to marry sometime before you're dead. Wouldn't you agree?

3. Now finish up your timeline test by adding the years next to your possessions. Granted, some items cost a lot more than others and might take longer to save for or attain, but ballparking where those items fall on your list will give you a sense of how to plan for them in terms of your timeline.

4. Sit back and take a look at your list. Are there any surprises? Does your timeline test accurately reflect a specific

time frame for each of your desired goals? Whatever your goal—landing a new job, finding a spouse, learning to speak Spanish or engaging in a spiritual practice—you now have a time-specific framework for making it happen.

5. Next, take a look at all your L list, or sometime-within-this-lifetime goals. Take a good look at those items and see if you want to give them a greater sense of urgency or if you're really okay with reaching them sometime, anytime, within your life. Unless that makes you move them up the priority scale, you may want to reconsider if they're really worth going after within the context of this book and, possibly, within the context of your life. Because you've got bigger fish to fry and more immediate goals to tackle.

Building momentum is all about streamlining. That's why you have to define your goals, add some realistic dates, and then drop off the excess baggage that's clouding up your thinking and slowing down your progress. Now that you've separated the important stuff from the surplus baggage, you can start putting some power behind the achieveable goals and letting momentum take its hold. Just like the insightful Toni Morrison quote at the head of this chapter, "Wanna fly, you got to give up the shit that weighs you down." Couldn't have said it more elegantly myself.

Of course, I encourage you to use the 3 P's and timeline test tools on an ongoing basis to help you continue to refocus your goals and adjust your priorities. In fact, by the time you read this, I might be jumping out of airplanes or running for public office. You never know!

Just so you can see how this works, let's take a look at the goals from my 3 P's list now that I've taken the timeline test.

Just as you did, I've put the number of years in which I want to accomplish each goal—one, three, five, ten—next to each item. My "within this lifetime" goals never even made the list since I am committed to focusing on things that I can accomplish within the next decade.

Here's what my timeline looked like:

PROFESSIONAL

Continue to build my business	1 year
Hire great people	1 year
Increase my earnings	1 year
Buy apartment/condo building	3 years
Write a new nonfiction book	1 year
Launch a syndicated self-help column	3 years
Build my speaking business	1 year
Have a radio show	5 years
Write a novel	5 years
Assist others in creating nontraditional businesses	5 years
Create a secondary business	10 years

PERSONAL

Spend lots of time with my kids	1 year (always)
Find a husband and get married again	1 year
Get personal trainer and get in shape	1 year
Take salsa or ballroom dance lessons	3 years
Take kids to Europe	1 year
Go to the Amazon	3 years
Find a spiritual community that's a good fit for me	1 year
Make home improvements	1 year
Convert garage to guest house	5 years
Relandscape	3 years
Learn to play tennis	3 years
Get scuba certified	1 year

Lose ten pounds	1 year
Research retirement homes	5 years

POSSESSIONS

Diamond ring (to go with husband)	1 year
Pickup truck for my gardening stuff	3 years
Collection of original California art	5 years
Some first editions	10 years
A real CD collection	1 year
A real CD player instead of the junk I have	1 year
Good computer system	3 years
"Media room" for kids	3 years
"Teenager" furniture for kids' rooms	3 years
New wardrobe (for newly trained figure)	1 year
Retirement property or house	10 years
Okay, I admit it, the boy's vintage Rolex watch	10 years

Wow! I've got a lot of work to do if I'm going to accomplish all those things in the next decade. Rather than getting completely overwhelmed at the enormity of that task, I'd rather take comfort in the fact that in just a couple of chapters, I'll be able to break all those goals down into doable action steps. I guess it's no wonder why the kids in high school teased me about dragging my calendar, Filofax, and to-do list everywhere I went. Even now, my friends refer to me as "the girl with the plan." Since you know my theory on tagging your baggage and then flipping it over to the positive side, you can bet that I consider being known as "the girl with the plan" a supreme compliment.

SUMMARY: SAND, ROCKS, AND WATER

There's an old story about a man who was assigned the task of filling a big glass jar with some large rocks, a bunch of sand, and a pitcher full of water. Don't ask me why people get hit with all these strange tasks in old stories, okay? They just do! When he put the sand in first, he found that he couldn't fit the rocks in around the sand. And when he put the water in first, it made it hard to get all the sand and rocks into the jar. But when he put the rocks in first, then packed the sand in around the rocks, then poured the water over the rocks and the sand—miraculously—it all fit in together.

The secret? When he started with the rocks—the big stuff—everything else had to find its own place around the periphery, which, somehow, it did. Just like life. If you start with the sand or the water, the little stuff, you will definitely take up all the volume—the time or focus or energy—that you have. And you won't have any room left over for the big rocks—your big-picture goals.

That's what discovering the power of the 3 P's is all about—defining the professional and personal milestones you want to hit and the possessions you want to own in order create the lifestyle you're longing to live. Once you've identified those, the next step in separating the dreamers from the do-ers is the timeline test, which puts a priority rank and level of urgency on each goal.

The two tools you have just completed are the beginning of your Traveling Hopefully Personal Road map. Just like the Chutes and Ladders game we discussed in the beginning of this chapter, your path can be fraught with peril. You are bound to backslide, stumble, and lose hope from time to time. Why not learn to be appropriately selfish so you can take care of yourself during those inevitable setbacks?

In chapter nine, we're going to learn that it's okay if it's all about me once in a while. Sure, it's great to be there for your family, your friends, your boss, your employees, but not all the time and at your own expense. You'll also learn a step-by-step process for recruiting your own customized Support Squad, who can give you the information and inspiration you need to keep up the momentum as you transform your life. Get ready to enjoy the downhill glide!

9

Eye of the Hurricane

*Combat Your Chaos Through
Selfishness and Support*

"What makes the desert beautiful is that somewhere
it hides a well."

—Antoine-Marie-Roger de Saint-Exupéry

As a kid growing up in the peninsula state of Florida, I was always surrounded by water. Our house sat alongside the banks of the St. Johns River, our city was bordered by the Atlantic Ocean, and our vacations were spent on the Gulf of Mexico. Hurricanes were, inevitably, a part of the natural landscape.

My client Angela, also a Southerner, had grown up along the coast of North Carolina. After completing graduate school with a master's degree in political science and public administration, she was offered a much sought-after position working with the governor's staff in a neighboring state. Angela had weathered coastal storms before, but her personal hurricanes were just beginning when she sought my guidance for what she thought would be a career transition.

Initially, Angela felt she'd achieved her goal of working for a powerful political machine and enacting meaningful change in people's lives, when she started to realize her dream job was actually a nightmare of infighting and backbiting. She had assumed lawmakers and politicians were above that sort of behavior, and found herself disheartened with the conduct of her colleagues and disappointed by the tedium of her low-level job. After so much time and hard work focused on a career in politics, Angela was facing total disillusionment and wondering if she should simply start all over again with a different career goal.

As we began to explore Angela's life themes to determine an appropriate course of action, she suffered a major setback. Angela was diagnosed with epilepsy. Suddenly she was adding serious concerns about her health and emotional well-being to her job worries. At first, Angela was plagued with fears about missing work and no longer being able to handle the heavy workload to which she'd been accustomed and others had come to expect. But when news of Angela's diagnosis circulated through the office, her colleagues—the very ones she had previously considered so difficult—rallied around her, offering support from helping out on her projects to offering her rides to the doctor, or stopping by her apartment with home-cooked casseroles. The unexpected side effect of Angela's devastating setback was finding a support team right in her backyard.

In chapter nine, we'll look at the art of appropriate selfishness and soliciting support, both of which serve as refuge from the storms of our chaotic lives. Maybe you find yourself combating that chaos every day or maybe you manage to keep to the eye of the storm most of the time. Wherever you are on the spectrum of calm to chaos, you can take advantage of specific methods to keep you on track and moving toward your goals, despite the stress that often accompanies change. The chaos that sometimes comes with life transformation may be unwelcome and unwanted, like hurricanes, but it is also predictable, so let's get prepared by learning the value of selfishness and support.

YOUR SUPPORT SQUAD

Part of positioning yourself for success—and a core belief of virtually every successful person on the planet—is that you cannot reach your goals alone. Step Three to Jumpstart Your Life is what I call recruiting a Support Squad; that is, a customized support system to help get you where you want to go. Critical to keeping you marching forward as well as overcoming the inevitable setbacks you'll experience, your Support Squad will provide you with emotional support, professional guidance, and ongoing inspiration. If you don't have a single solitary person cheering you on from the sidelines or aiding you in your quest for a more satisfying life, don't worry. You've got me, and I'm just the start of your support team. By the time you finish this chapter, you will be able to identify, solicit, and lead the Support Squad that you will have handpicked and recruited specifically to help you reach your goals.

You can't recruit, much less lead, a squad if you're not willing to be in charge. Don't panic, leading your team does not require prior experience as a CEO or an army general, it just requires that you learn to put yourself first. That's why the tools and exercises in this chapter—recruiting your Support Squad, it's all about me, and the life launcher—are designed to teach you how to be appropriately selfish so you can accept the support you deserve.

I'm going to go way out on a limb and venture a wild guess that *you* are probably hovering somewhere near the very bottom of your to-do list right now; that is, assuming you even appear on your list at all. I dare you to check it out right this very minute. If you're a list-maker, calendar-keeper, or PDA person, get out your to-do list and total up how many action items are on your calendar to benefit other people — including your boss, kids, spouse, friends, neighbors — and how many action items are there solely for the care and nurturing of you. If you're like most of us, you probably don't make yourself a priority — either on your to-do list or in your life. Before you can even think about building a support system, you've got to start thinking about you. That's why the following tool, it's all about me, is all about you.

Tool # 17: It's All About Me

If you're like me, your life is consumed by other people's needs. No matter how good a juggler you are, once you factor in work, family, and friends, there's very little time left over for you. And I'm just talking about taking time for the basics: your emotional health, physical wellness, and relaxation. At this point, we're not even considering the time you'll need in order to bring your big picture vision to life — the one you've begun to create as you've worked through the last eight chapters. If it's hard to find some free time to get the gym or watch a movie, imagine how selfish you're going to have to be if you want to make the sweeping changes that will get you to the more joyful existence you've been actively envisioning. Even taking the time to read this book may have felt incredibly selfish to you, but it all goes back to perspective, as we discussed in chapter five when we looked at your half-empty/half-full life. When you take time to improve your health, increase your energy, reduce your stress, and learn new skills, you are moving toward a more joyful life. You're Traveling Hopefully. And you'll be taking other people with you, even if they don't do a thing to change their lives. As your life changes—as you become more fit, energetic, and joyful—the lives of the people you love will also change, simply because they're in the presence of a more balanced you who has more to offer.

In the last chapter, we talked about identifying your goals, creating a timetable, and streamlining your priorities so you could focus on the important stuff. Well, nothing qualifies as more important than you. It's like the airline safety advisory— "Put the oxygen mask on yourself first, then help others." If you pass out from lack of oxygen, you're not much good to your family, your friends, your boss, or anyone else. So let's talk specifics of it's all about me. Here's what I want you to do:

1. Give that area in your home or office that you've claimed as your Hopeful Tool healing sanctuary or meditation zone a more personal name or label, one that inspires and encourages you and links this spot with all the positive changes you've made and will continue to make. You might call it your sanctuary, your favorite place, your meditation room, or your comfort spot. Whatever is an appealing reminder that you deserve a special place. Now place a special item in the space that will designate it as your special healing place, like a favorite candle or vase. In this way, you'll be making your meditation zone sacrosanct— at least for a few minutes a day.

2. Relax, clear your mind and take out your Traveling Hopefully Daybook or a piece of paper. Now, instead of writing "to do" on the top of your list, write "It's All About Me."

3. List seven things you can do that would be all about you. Not about your kids, your boss, your pets, your spouse,

your mother, or your next-door neighbor. Just about you. The idea of listing seven things is to get your ideas flowing so you can envision a range of activities that would bring joy into your life. They might include:

- A trip to a museum
- A walk or a hike in a beautiful natural setting
- A movie, maybe all by yourself in the middle of the afternoon
- Making time for a favorite hobby
- Taking a leisurely drive
- A street fair or cultural event
- A splurge—dinner out or tickets to a concert or play

If it's difficult to wrap your brain around seven things that are all about you, try filling in the blank: "I'd really like to—." Make some of these immediate, easily doable activities, others more long-range in nature. Some can include other people, but I want you to have at least four out of the seven that are solitary activities, because it's all about you, right? Go back to your list of personal goals from Tool #15 if you need some additional inspiration.

Here's my list:

IT'S ALL ABOUT ME!

1. Get a massage
2. Plan a vacation just for me
3. Plan a vacation for me and the kids
4. Buy fresh flowers for the office
5. Take a long walk
6. Take a bubble bath
7. Turn off the TV/talk radio and listen to music

Was it difficult to come up with seven activities devoted to you? I really bogged down once I got to item four. It was nearly impossible to get those last three items down on the page. Then I realized that I was only focusing on the major events like vacations and pampering sessions and overlooking the little, everyday things that I could easily give myself whenever I wanted to take a moment and recharge my batteries. That's when I thought back to the time I joined the ranks of the most stressed and least rested group on the planet — new parents.

Caring for a newborn is so time- and energy-consuming that caring for yourself, even on the most fundamental "Can I squeeze in a shower?" level, becomes secondary. The best survival techniques I ever learned, like "Nap when the baby naps" and "Forget about cleaning the house for the first few weeks" were gleaned from age-old maternal wisdom. What that sage advice also teaches parents is to rejoice in the moments, not just the hours, days, or weeks. If you're going to survive the often mind-numbing fatigue of new parenthood, you have to learn to revel in the five minutes you have for a quick shower, rejoice in a twenty-minute bubble bath, and celebrate the first time you sleep through the night. If you take that same approach and apply it every day whether you have a newborn or not, you'll find that those spare moments can really add up. If you use those moments to do what brings you joy — guess what — you'll start feeling more positive and then begin to find the time and energy for the sweeping changes that your life transformation will require.

Change, whether it's personal or professional, puts special demands on your schedule and your psyche. It's intense and emotional, and, like an athlete, you need to be in shape for it. Seize those moments for yourself and then learn to stretch them into hours, days, and weeks. Can you even conceive of a week spent doing exactly what you want to do? Maybe not, or at least not yet. Certainly you can come up with an hour's worth of activities that would make you happy.

"It's all about me" also means it's all about holding *me* accountable. Since you are now accountable for jumpstarting a life that brings you satisfaction and happiness, I'm going to ask you to add a timeline to your list. Here's what I want you to do: Pick one or two items on your list that you can accomplish within the next twenty-four hours. Pick three or four things you can do within the next week, and one or two things that you can do within the next month. Even if you can't necessarily complete the activity within a month, say going to Europe with your kids, you can start the planning process within the month. Are you ready to hold yourself accountable?

Here's my list with timetable:

It's All About Me with Time Frame

1. Get a massage	Within a week
2. Plan a vacation just for me	Within a month
3. Plan a vacation for me and the kids	Within a month
4. Buy fresh flowers for the office	Within a week
5. Take a long walk	Within 24 hours
6. Take a bubble bath	Within 24 hours
7. Turn off the TV and listen to music	Within a week

I actually found a couple of things I could do today—a long walk and a bubble bath. If I get lucky, my walk might take me past a flower stand as it did yesterday where I walked right past a beautiful five-dollar bouquet, convinced I shouldn't spend that money on myself. I love flowers, and the fact that I would deny myself a five-dollar bouquet, especially since I would have bought it for someone else in a heartbeat, is just plain ridiculous. Somehow, even when I can well afford it, I've trained myself into a life of self-denial. It takes writing down your it's all about me list—and holding yourself accountable—to make you do what you said you would do in service of yourself.

Okay, I'm off to take a walk, buy a bouquet of flowers, and then take a long bubble bath. Not bad for an hour!

THE LIFE LAUNCHER

Once my recurring life theme of "You're in this alone" began to fade into the background, the idea of building my own customized support team became more and more attractive. I could almost feel the momentum build as my team coached me from the sidelines, the baby steps coming more swiftly and easily as I moved toward my big goals. I dreamed of a retreat at some fancy hotel, just like the ones I'd attended in my corporate days, only this one wouldn't be dedicated to restructuring the organization, but to restructuring my life. As I pictured the people I wanted sitting around the board table and weighing in at this imaginary event devoted to me, I considered the different aspects of my life I'd want my dream team to address.

The life launcher is an exercise which, when completed, will give you a graphic representation of the key areas of your life that are most important to you, then allow you to stack them up in priority order to see where you feel you are most successful. Like many of the tools you've already explored, this is another way to help you determine what kind of life you want to live and how to get it.

In a moment you'll identify the key aspects that you consider most important to your life. For now, take a look at the list below to give you some ideas.

- Family
- Romantic relationship

- Friendships
- Fitness and physical well-being
- Fun and adventure
- Career
- Money
- Home
- Education
- Spiritual growth
- Personal growth
- Creative endeavors
- Add any items of your own

Now pick all the items from this list, including any you've added, that you feel are important to living a life of purpose and passion. If "family" and "career" are important to you, put them on your list. If "creative endeavors" or "education" aren't important to you, drop them. Write out your list in your Traveling Hopefully Daybook.

Next to each item you've listed, put a percentage number up to 100 percent that shows how you'd grade yourself in that area of your life in terms of having achieved what you want. In other words, if you feel you are successful in your family life, you might grade yourself 90 percent. On the other hand, if you are flunking out in "fun and adventure," you might score yourself a 35 percent.

My life launcher list looks like this:

Family	70%
Friendships	85%
Romantic relationship	30%
Fun and adventure	20%
Career	85%
Home	75%
Money	80%
Spiritual growth	65%

Now let's turn this into a graphic snapshot via the life launcher ladder. Draw two parallel vertical lines several inches apart down the page of your daybook, then draw lines across linking them together, like a ladder. Now on each horizontal line, or rung in the ladder, write in the name of an item on your list. Start with those with the highest scores — items in which you feel you are attaining your goals — at the bottom, and those items with the lowest scores — where you need to focus and improve — at the top.

Chances are if you're like most of us, you've got a high-scoring item or two that serves as your foundation, the bottom rungs on your ladder. Toward the top of your life launcher, your ladder gets a little shakier. That's where you may want to focus time and energy. In addition to being a great visual device to help you determine where you need to be more selfish, the life launcher is a starting point for deciding what you want your Support Squad to help you with. Starting today, look around you and begin to take note of all the people out there who just might be willing to enlist in your cause. In a moment, we'll talk more about the specifics of the three-pronged process — identifying, soliciting, and giving back — involved in building your squad of supporters.

CLIMBING THE SAND DUNE

There's a sand dune not far from my house. It's not right on the beach but about ten blocks inland in a park called, aptly enough, Sand Dune Park. The dune is a steep sand hill about ten stories high, and lots of people come there to work out with their stopwatch-toting trainers or to play with their kids, who love to sled down the dune on trash can lids.

One day I was climbing the hill when I noticed a group of girls ahead of me. There were about twenty of them huffing and puffing their way up toward the summit. They appeared to be fifteen or sixteen years old, and I noticed they had on T-shirts with church logos for some congregation or youth group. As I got a little closer, I saw that each girl was carrying one of those big, gray concrete cinder blocks up the hill. As they climbed, in little clumps of twos and threes, the stronger girls were cheering the others on, yelling out tips on breathing and admonishing the stragglers not to give up.

When I got up to the summit, I saw that as each girl got to the top, she would drop her cinder block, turn and run—free and unencumbered—right back down to the bottom of the dune, where she'd grab another block, turn and start her climb all over again. I watched this delightful aerobic ballet unfold in front of me, thinking how lovely it was that these young women were carrying their burdens together, the stronger ones leading the way one foot in front of the other, all of them feeding off each other's energy and encouragement.

I realized that my climb was much less arduous than usual. I looked down and saw that I was following in these girls' footsteps. I realized how much easier it was climbing up that dune when I could get a foothold instead of fighting the shifting sands as I usually did. I kept climbing upward, stepping in their footsteps, and noticed that there were more girls coming up behind me, stepping in mine. This was the very essence of support—having someone on your team who's already traveled your path and can help you to find your footing and ease your climb to the summit.

There was a certain southern California poetry in watching that group of young women in the bright summer sunshine cheering each other on as they charged the crest of that sand dune. Clearly, they had created an effective support system, with the whole group dedicated to getting each other to the top. But what if you're not part of a ready-made team? What if you're a solo act, anxious to build a Support

Squad but unsure where to start? Or maybe you've never even considered how instrumental a team approach can be in shortening your growth curve and getting you where you want to go. That's about to change, so consider me your first squad member!

Tool # 18: Recruiting Your Support Squad

As I mentioned, recruiting your Support Squad requires a three-pronged approach, as follows:

- Decide what type of team you need. Determine the personality types or expertise you need in your Support Squad to help you reach your predetermined goals. You can do this by determining the type of function you want fulfilled or by identifying a specific person, possibly someone you already know, as a potential recruit, even if you're not yet sure what his or her function will be. If this all sounds clinical or manipulative, trust me, it won't be once you've mastered the next step.

- Learn to communicate your needs. Let potential Support Squad members know exactly the type of help you want. Then graciously let them off the hook if they're not interested or available. We'll practice that conversation in a moment.

- Give back to your support team. Repay the emotional support, guidance, and help your squad has so generously given you in any form that is meaningful to them—or to their friends, family, or colleagues.

Remember the lesson I learned from the script librarian who wanted to help me, but whose noble intentions were thwarted by my lack of openness to her support? Most people get great satisfaction from helping others—and those are the type of people you want to recruit into your army. But not everyone is willing or able to help you. That's why making it clear that this is a request and not a demand will let you both walk away with your relationship intact, even if you hit an impasse.

As I moved from the corporate into the entrepreneurial world—producing, consulting, and coaching—I found myself constantly faced with new challenges. It seemed every time I attended a meeting or even picked up the phone, I was involved in an entirely new scenario. All these firsts were exhilarating, but also exhausting. I needed help—and that's where my squad, sometimes with reinforcements, came to the rescue.

In the early stages of formulating what later became my Traveling Hopefully Personal Road map, I had kept a list on my laptop of people who I thought would consider helping me in my quest for life change. Some I knew personally and some I knew only by reputation. In addition to names, I also kept a list of functions, like job titles, that highlighted distinct areas in which I knew I needed expertise or support. This list—by name and function—eventually evolved into my Support Squad.

As my life and needs changed, so did my team. Some people, like Andy, my former boss, signed on for early mentorship and never left. Others joined voluntarily or allowed me to recruit them along the way, as my professional and personal needs came into ever sharper focus and I recognized the type of support I needed. Suddenly, I experienced karmic payback for all the favors I'd done for others over the years. People just kept popping up to support me.

With Andy and my gifted therapist, Nancy, on board, my fledgling army was born. Now, I was ready to build on my strengths, shore up my weaknesses, and move toward the goals I'd already set for myself. Some honest self-assessment of my own limitations led me to the conclusion that the next order of business would be to find someone to help me manage my money. I was pretty good at making it, very good at helping others make it, but I knew if I were to accomplish my goals, I needed to become a smarter financial manager. I sought out new recruits in the form of business managers Mike, Terry, and Michelle, professionals whom I paid for their expertise just as I did my therapist. My Support Squad began to take shape and build momentum.

Here's what my early Support Squad wish list looked like. I've listed them by their function and broken them down into specific sub-groups. I didn't expect or need all these people on my squad, but it was a great way to focus on the type of support I wanted. The people I recruited for their general support and guidance, like my old boss who was supportive even before I knew exactly what I needed his support for, later served one or more of those functions.

Support Squad wish list:

- Emotional Support—skilled therapist, loving friends, single women, people with kids
- Parenting Support—pediatrician, teachers and school guidance counselors, friends who are parents
- Financial Counsel—trusted family members with financial savvy; business managers and accountants
- Professional Advice in Business Strategy—business mentor/friend, agent, attorney
- Professional Advice in Creative Endeavors—producing partner, literary mentor, agent
- Physical Training, Advice, and Care—trainer, doctors, chiropractor, best friend/workout partner

- Spiritual Guidance—minister, rabbi, pastoral counselor
- Home Care and Improvement—gardener, cleaning service, handyman/plumber

I still use this list as a guideline to help me determine the type of support I need, but now there are several names attached to each function. I also use the list to evaluate how effectively my support system is operating within their previously defined roles, how well it's serving my current needs, and if I'm appropriately giving back to my team members. Sometimes the names change, often people opt out based on their own needs and schedules. Occasionally, I add a new function or specialty to the list or take one off, but I always find that if I clearly define the type of support I am seeking, whether it's an orthodontist for my son's braces or some single women friends that like to travel, if I can articulate to myself what I want and need, it's much easier to articulate it to others.

What about your own support needs? What are the functions you need your Support Squad to perform? Do you have a circle of friends, business associates, or mentors from which you might begin to build a team of supporters for whatever you need, from information to inspiration? Can you think of five or six people who might be willing to help you accomplish your goals? Where might you find the people who could be potential recruits for your Support Squad?

Here's what I want you do:

BUILDING YOUR SUPPORT SQUAD
BY FUNCTION OR PERSON

1. Make a list of all the functions that you'd like represented in your Support Squad. Look back at my wish list to get an idea of what your list might include. Although I've

listed a lot of different options under each heading, including some that require payment, you may not need more than one person, including a friend or unpaid advisor, in each category. Include descriptions that cover your goals in business, spirituality, education, personal growth, fitness, fun and recreation, etc. Make sure you customize this list to fit your specific needs, whether they are related to your personal health, hobbies, plans to start your own company—whatever makes your plan unique to you.

2. Next, make a list of all the people you know personally or know of whom you would like to have on your team. Aim high, but be realistic. It's unlikely that you'll get Steven Spielberg, Bill Gates, or Oprah Winfrey on your team, but you can list someone who fulfills that role even if they're not quite that high up the food chain. If you can't come up with a name, simply write "creative mentor" or "business whiz," or "workout buddy," or whatever function you're interested in having that squad member perform.

3. Now go back to steps one and two above. If you've listed a function but don't have the actual person to fulfill it yet, start to brainstorm names of people who might be willing to take on that role or point you toward someone who could. For example, if you pinpointed "financial advisor" as a function need, start to list some people or business organizations who can help you find that team member. Conversely, if you listed people who you think might be willing to serve on your support team, add some details next to their names as to what function you think they can fulfill. You put their names down for a reason, now think about how they'd best serve you. Remember "it's all about me"? This is selfish time, don't fight it.

Asking for help is all about the positioning. So let's position you to recruit your Support Squad successfully by learning to communicate your needs effectively but graciously to the people you're lining up. Feel free to practice on a spouse or trusted friend so that you become fluent in the language of asking for help and giving the recruit an opportunity to gracefully decline. Here goes:

RECRUITING YOUR SUPPORT SQUAD BY SIMULTANEOUSLY ASKING FOR HELP AND LETTING THE RECRUIT OFF THE HOOK

1. Explain to your potential Support Squad member, in simple terms, what you are trying to accomplish and how he or she can help you reach that goal. For example, "Hi, Business Mentor/Friend, I am planning to open my own business within the next three years, and I could really use some ongoing advice about the competitive landscape, structuring a start-up, etc."

2. Next, define that person's role, open to negotiation, of course, and—in the next breath—graciously let the person you are trying to recruit off the hook. Like so: "And Business Mentor/Friend, I'm wondering if you'd be willing to have breakfast with me every couple of months, at your convenience, to give me some ongoing guidance. Of course, if your time is too limited, I understand and would be delighted if you could recommend someone else who might be willing to fulfill this function for me."

Remember the role-playing of critical conversations that we did in the last chapter? This is a good time to practice using that skill. Trust me, asking for help gets easier each time you do it.

Obviously, your tone will be dictated by how well you know this person and the nature of your relationship, whether you are asking a friend for a favor or if this is a business solicitation for which you expect to pay the other party. But don't underestimate how many people you already know or can find—in PTA, at your local business clubs or organizations, or through night school or college courses—who will provide these services for little or no cost. Even if this is an agent, attorney, coach or other professional advisor whom you plan to pay, it's still beneficial if they understand that you require ongoing guidance that may be beyond the bounds of other more traditional clients and that they are part of a larger system of support. Ask and you might get, don't ask and you definitely don't get.

When I decided that I wanted to leave my corporate job, I bounced my idea of writing and providing corporate and personal coaching services off my former boss, Andy. Without hesitation, he offered to help. In retrospect, I could see that he thought I was crazy to throw away a corporate entertainment career for something that I couldn't yet articulate, but he sensed the passion and fervor with which I was attempting to change the direction of my professional and personal life. After he said he'd be happy to help me, I asked him what his desire to help meant. Could we have breakfast once a month or so, until I had some sense of direction? Could I call him when I was in crisis or needed help with a big decision? Yes, he told me, we could have breakfast once a month, and he would bring along associates from time to time who could be helpful to my progress. And yes, I could call him, but not only when I was in crisis. Anytime I needed anything, big or small, period. And he meant every word of it.

I feel as if the twenty years of favors I've done for people— helping them find jobs, reading and editing their pitches, coaching them through career and personal transitions—has more than been paid back in the past few years alone. I provided those mentoring services for free long before I did professionally, just as people later did for me. Once I discovered the power of asking for help in a clear and conscious way, defining the terms and conditions of that help, then letting people have a graceful out if they didn't have the time, inclination, or resources to sign up, my life changed in the most profound and dramatic ways.

When I try to move forward to conquer a new goal or to complete an ongoing task, my Support Squad is there. When I hit a snag or setback, a round of phone calls to a member of my support system can set me right back on course with a minimum of angst or stewing in the problem. Whether it's business savvy, a pat on the back, or the inside track to someone or something I need, one of my squad members usually has the info.

I hope this is obvious, but just in case it's not, I always try to be as available and helpful to my Support Squad as they are to me. It's never a tit for tat, quid pro quo kind of relationship, it's whatever they need, whenever they need it, no questions asked. Because that's how much they mean to me.

SUMMARY: IT'S ALL ABOUT US

When I first contemplated launching my own company, I worried that every brainstorming meeting or networking dinner was time away from my family. Even though I was beginning to build a solid plan and a strong support system, I couldn't handle the feelings of selfishness that overwhelmed me. Finally, going back to my verbal meditations, I mapped out exactly the kind of life I would have when I hit these career milestones I was beginning to see very clearly. I saw how the financial freedom and the ability to dictate my own schedule would soon be of great benefit to my children, who would soon get a lot more of me. Selfishness was a trade-off but not a sacrifice, and certainly not a hardship. Suddenly, it wasn't all about me—it was all about us.

Remember the great Oscar Wilde comedy *The Importance of Being Earnest*, which you probably read in tenth grade English? In this chapter, we learned not about the importance of earnestness, but the importance of selfishness, because what good are you to anyone else if you're overtired, overstressed, and unable to accomplish the goals that will directly affect your life and those of everyone around you? By recruiting a Support Squad, you can achieve those goals much faster and with more joyfulness than you ever could if you were operating in isolation. In chapter ten, we'll talk about being "in the flow," or in your creative element, and you'll discover how you can expand your thinking about reaching your goals as well as leading your team to help you create the life of passion and purpose that you deserve.

10

In the Flow

Tapping in to and Trusting Your Creative Spirit

"The moment of change is the only poem."
—**Adrienne Rich**

What if we could get the guidance we're seeking simply by opening our channels of creativity? What if the help, resources, or love of our life really does show up because we've tapped into our own creative inspiration to ask for it? What if we could fulfill, or even surpass, our boldest dreams? That's powerful stuff.

Creativity is the experience of letting the divine flow through you. Of really getting out of the way, shutting off whatever part of you — doubt, fear, pragmatism — needs to be tuned out in order for some other spirit to take over. What is your biggest fear about tapping into your own creativity? Is it that you're not creative? Is it that you'll become some sort of deranged artist if you let your intuition take over? Is it that you'll be ridiculed or judged by others? Or is it that you'll unleash some powerful part of yourself and never be the same again?

Maybe you've had the feeling that you were creatively blocked, emotionally burned out, or that everything and everyone in your world was intent on stifling your spirit? In chapter ten, we're going to let go of everything you've learned so far and invite that creative spirit back in to our lives. Don't think all your hard work has been in vain, even though I'm asking you to put it aside for now. Trust that your subconscious has already internalized all the homework you've done and, like a computer file, you'll be able to access it precisely when you need it. Your powers of internal clarity have sharpened considerably as you've worked your way through the first eighteen Hopeful Tools in this book. Now we're going to tap into something even bigger than your own inner voice. We're about to access the collective consciousness of the universe. Relax and imagine the right side of your brain, the creative side, opening up and allowing the creative spirit to flow through you.

If you're thinking that creativity is reserved for artists, designers, writers, and other esoteric types lurking around garrets or galleries, you're defining the word too narrowly. Creativity encompasses more than the traditional artistic pursuits. We're defining creativity as a way of thinking or traveling hopefully through the world as an open vessel, allowing guidance and inspiration to flow in from many sources, even those that are sometimes unseen. Learning to trust your creative instincts isn't an abstract exercise in aesthetics. It's a practical way to solve problems and to find new perspectives and solutions for everything from parenting and relationship issues to professional dilemmas. Tapping into your creativity isn't a question of sitting around waiting for that zap of creative juice to start coursing through your veins like a rush of adrenaline. As counterintuitive as it may seem, you have more control of your own creativity than you may think. You just have to learn how to tune in and let go.

Scott was a boutique owner who wanted my help because he couldn't seem to get his small design store past a certain threshold of productivity. Despite the fact that Scott's business of selling custom-designed furniture required that he work very closely with highly creative designers and skilled craftsmen, Scott never considered himself a creative thinker. Convinced that he had a marketing or staffing problem but unable to put his finger on its exact nature, he came to me for guidance. It soon became clear that Scott had no vision of what he wanted to accomplish, either in his professional or personal life. Consequently, his store was stagnating and the quality of his family life was diminishing.

Scott told me he had originally come to Los Angeles to be a screenwriter but after marrying a makeup artist and having two children, he'd put that dream aside and opened his store in a fashionably funky part of Hollywood. As Scott began tapping into his internal vision using tools like meeting the future self and verbal meditation, he found his creative juices beginning to flow. By writing out reactions to these exercises in his daybook, Scott was able to recognize a recurring theme of which he was barely aware.

Scott realized he was carrying on a continuous internal dialogue about whether he should sell the store and move his family back to Minneapolis where he could join his brother in his manufacturing business. Suddenly, it became clear to him why his boutique had failed to thrive. Armed with the realization that Scott's ambivalence was sabotaging his success, he determined that he would put his doubts on hold, continue to build the boutique for three more years, then assess whether or not it was time to sell. In the meantime, Scott redirected his creative energies into marketing and staffing improvements and watched his sales soar.

Tool # 19: Unlocking Your Creative Spirit

I have a friend who not only insists on carrying his eighteen-month-old son in a baby backpack, but, on occasion, setting him up on top of the refrigerator or in the branch of a tree, all with a stabilizing parental hand. He believes it provides his child with a fresh perspective and a different outlook on the world, especially since his son's viewpoint is mostly ankle down.

Did you ever have a teacher who suggested holding a class lecture outside under a tree? Or a boss who wanted to have a brainstorming session at the beach? Maybe, like that little guy in the backpack, you've noticed that you can think more creatively when you're at a sidewalk café watching the world go by or pulling weeds in your backyard, rather than sitting at same old desk facing the same old computer screen. Just shaking up your routine can get you into a different frame of mind, allowing those creative problem-solving skills to kick in and solutions to bubble up to the surface. Let's experiment with some different ways to unlock your creativity. Here's what I want you to do.

1. Go to your meditation zone, which, by now, you've claimed as your own. Start your deep breathing or other stress-releasing exercises to begin to get into the creative flow. Pay special attention to your inner dialogue and ease up as much as possible on any critical messages. Instead, substitute some kind words for yourself about your willingness to take a risk, to continue trying out new tools and perspectives, and to seek ways to bring more passion and

purpose into your life. In other words, give yourself a big pat on the back for not giving up on you.

2. Next, look at the following list of creativity-inducing activities designed to get you out of your rational mind and into a creative state. I want you to try each one of them and record your reactions in your Traveling Hopefully Daybook. If you can't do all of them right away, pick one that you will do within twenty-four hours, one that you'll do within the next week, and one that you will do within a month. We've discussed the importance of momentum, so don't let your pace falter now. It's up to you to hold yourself accountable for completing each activity, or join forces with a trusted friend or partner to hold each other accountable. Whatever gets the job done.

Start a dream diary. Keep track of your dreams for a designated period of time, remembering your dreams when you awaken in the morning. Record what happens in your dream and what it means to you. As with verbal meditation, it's best to record your impressions as soon as you wake up, before the conscious mind blots out your dream images. There's a reason for the old saying that in order for your dreams to come true, you have to tell them before breakfast. Keeping track of your dreams can help you see your life in a more free-flowing, less linear way, opening up a new channel to your inner creativity. You may see meaningful symbols emerge as you become more adept at remembering and interpreting images. You may even be able to steer your dreams, setting up scenarios before you go to sleep and getting solutions via your dream symbols that you can record in your daybook the next morning.

Paint your masterpiece. Indulge your artistic fantasy. Whether you see yourself as a Renoir or a Pollock, get out your water-colors, oils, easel, canvas or butcher paper, and create a work of art. If you're used to drawing with chalk or pencils, don't. This is the time to try something new. It doesn't matter if it's splatter technique or still life, but let yourself get lost in the moment and see what develops. Try a few different media, or go to different settings or try drawing or painting at different times of the day. What do you think of your art? How did you feel when you created it? Record your feelings in your daybook.

Form a drum circle. Get together with a group of friends and make some noise with rhythm instruments. Discover the incredible sense of community that comes from making music, even primitive music, together. If the spirit moves you, get up and dance to the beat.

Take a hike. Literally, that is. Try taking a walk through an unfamiliar part of town or in a natural setting. Be sure to focus all your senses on your surroundings, taking in sights, sounds, and smells as you travel.

Create a comic book. Be a kid again and create your own comic book heroes and villains, then illustrate your storyline with words and pictures. You can do it the good old-fashioned way, on notebook paper folded in half and stapled along the edge like a book or on colored construction paper if you want a little pizzazz. Who knows? You might just be the next Stan Lee, the man who created Spider-man and my younger son's personal creative hero.

Discover the zen of window washing. Pick a chore that requires repetitive action, preferably one where you can see your results, like window washing, painting a fence, or mopping a floor. Complete your task on autopilot, letting your mind relax and wander. Not only do you get into a zen state, you get a chore completed to boot!

To test my own theory on letting creativity flow, I decided to attack a work problem with which I was grappling by choosing one of the activities from the list above. I decided to put my problem — how to prepare and position a client for a particularly challenging media event — on the mental back burner as I tackled my creative endeavor. Always up for a challenge, I picked painting as the activity that felt the least comfortable to me. I got out the watercolors and brushes that I'd bought at the neighborhood office supply store and painted my masterpiece of the magnolia tree in my front yard. Okay, so I'm not exactly Georgia O'Keeffe, but it wasn't too bad either. Best of all, it was thoroughly relaxing to check out of my usual thought patterns and get into the creative flow. Sure enough, by the time I got back to my desk, it was as though the freedom of painting my magnolias had spilled over into my work and I found the perfect solution for my problem client.

I'll tackle the comic book this week and the dream diary within the month. I might even add knitting to my list since it's something I used to love because it got me into a rhythmic meditative state. Is there a knitting equivalent in your past? Feel free to add any other activities to your list that unleash your sense of creativity. Next, we're going to talk about how unlocking creativity can unlock your life, especially when you're feeling stuck and solutionless.

LETTING GO OF OUTCOMES

Mitch came to me for personal coaching because he couldn't figure out how to connect his dream of being a comedy writer to his current life as a marketing consultant for a cosmetics company. No matter how he sliced and diced it, he just couldn't see any sort of progression from cosmetics to comedy. Mitch was a wildly creative guy, even if no one knew it but us! Trusting my own creative instincts, I sensed that we had to get him out of himself in order to find himself.

As Mitch began to work on linking up internal clarity with external action, it became clear that he was having difficulty connecting with his own creative instincts. He was stuck on the outcome—the killer of creative thought—and couldn't see anything but the big score as an established Hollywood comedy writer. Granted, you need to determine your end goal, but you also have to recognize the steps that are within your control and that you can make happen, as well as the areas over which you have no control. The point is to do your best work and then let go of the outcome, because there are no guarantees. Even if you do everything the way you've mapped it out, your plan for reaching your goal can still crash and burn. If you define failure as I do, a learning lesson, then you're still moving toward your goal. Mitch was getting completely hung up on the result—the part that is not within his control—and ignoring his creative process.

Mitch and I focused on his action steps by putting external pieces, like his Support Squad, in place. Simultaneously, he continued to build internal clarity, starting with creating his healing sanctuary. He'd taken over the basement of his old house and turned it into a recording studio. Music, particularly playing the guitar, was what got Mitch back into his creative zone. Though there might not seem to be a direct link between music and comedy, for Mitch there was. Once he began writing songs, everything started falling into place. By making music and tapping into his creative instincts, Mitch built up the level of trust and confidence that allowed him to take the required risks in his comedy performance.

Most important, he stopped focusing on the outcome and began to focus on his own actions.

Since Mitch often acted as emcee at the huge trade shows his company attended to market their line of products, we concocted a plan for him to do a stand-up comedy routine instead of his usual executive introductions. Who better to spoof the world of beauty than a guy who knew that world inside and out? So Mitch, with the blessing of his boss, put together a three-minute opening monologue which positioned him as a likeable guy who had the guts to poke some good-natured fun at an industry ripe with comic potential. It was a risky move, especially since it exposed him to his colleagues, clients, and superiors in a completely different light. He went through with it, and, as they say in show biz, he killed!

Mitch brought down the house with his spot-on routine, and offers to perform at trade shows and to write comedy pieces for company newsletters poured in. It wasn't Hollywood, but it was a darn good start. Mitch took a calculated risk and leveraged his day job to get to his dream job. We'll discuss more about leveraging your current situation to move toward your goals in the last chapter. For right now, let's stay with trusting your creative instincts. Even though he was an incredibly imaginative guy, Mitch had become so focused on his ultimate goal of becoming a Hollywood comedy writer that the fear associated with attaining it shut him down. Had he not gotten back into music and rediscovered his creative energy, he might have lost out on a lot of exciting opportunities. Once he tapped into his artistic instincts, one creative baby step at a time, it all came together.

Even if you're not involved in anything as obviously "creative" as playing music or writing comedy, remember that every human being is born with a creative spirit. What do you think kept us alive all those centuries—facing man-eating saber-toothed tigers and raging blizzards, harnessing fire and designing tools? Creativity is survival at its most basic. Either our God-given instincts come to our rescue or we become somebody's dinner.

Maybe you're not buying any of this, maybe you see no value in creativity. Creative stuff is only for artists, not for regular folks who have kids, jobs, pets, broken water heaters to repair, and mortgages to pay. Creativity is self-indulgent and time-wasting crap, you say, so who needs it? But life does not have to equal drudgery. If your creative mind can tackle some of the problem-solving in the hard-core real world, then you can take care of business and still have some time and energy left over to build the kind of life you actually want, instead of the one the world handed to you and you neglected to hand back. Admit it, aren't you at least a little tired of running in place? So let's take a little of that creative energy you've unlocked a step further and see how it might apply to the way you think about work.

Tool # 20: Cash In on Your Passion

For the last ten chapters, you've been thinking about what you want your life, both personally and professionally, to look like. This particular tool offers ways to get that creative spirit flowing into your career. It's what I call cashing in on your passion, requiring you to locate the intersection of creativity and commerce. The idea here is not necessarily to solve all of your work-related problems, but to link up creativity with your working life.

Consider how a little creative inspiration might lead you toward good contacts or interesting projects, or just bring more opportunities your way. You need to get into a relaxed state, breathing deeply and letting stress melt away. Let go of negative judgments and try out each of these activities, recording your thoughts and feelings in your Traveling Hopefully Daybook. If you can't attack these all at once, give yourself a deadline for getting them done. Here goes:

- *Write your own professional obituary.* Think about the trade paper or journal that is most significant within your profession. If one doesn't exist, make one up or use your local newspaper. Now write your obituary for that publication, listing all your hoped-for professional accomplishments, accolades, and relationships. This exercise, like the scenario you imagined for your hundredth birthday party, will get you thinking about the life ahead of you. Only this time, it's in the context of your career or the career for which you hope to be remembered and honored.

- *Create a success collage.* Collect images — words and pictures — from different publications and create a cut-and-paste collage depicting your future career-related success. Start with a title or favorite quote that you make out of cut-out words, like those hokey ransom notes you see in old movies. Round up some magazines, get out the poster board and glue stick, and really have some fun with this one. Let the finished product inspire you to greatness!

- *Design a career history timeline.* Draw a timeline like the one you drew in fifth grade social studies class, but instead of pinpointing the important dates in American history, highlight all the significant dates, titles, and milestones — imagined or real — that you plan to hit as you move toward your big picture career goal. This will come in very handy as we turn everything you've done so far into your Traveling Hopefully Personal Road map in the next chapter.

Once you've had a chance to try a few of the above activities, ask yourself how they affected you. Were you surprised at any of your reactions? Did one particular method of getting into the creative flow work better for you than others? I first used the obituary exercise a couple of years ago, when I was coaching a young woman named Laura through what she called her "quarter-century crisis." Right after college, Laura had landed a job working as an assistant at a real estate brokerage and had been working there ever since. She liked the people, but as her dissatisfaction with the job itself began to grow and spill over into other parts of her life, Laura had to admit that she was just coasting along instead of charting her own course. Bit by bit, Laura felt she was losing all sense of balance and that the joy was draining out of her life.

When I suggested she write her professional obituary to see if it would shake up some creative spirit and shed some light on what she really wanted, she was skeptical but willing. Initially, she planned to write the obituary for a popular real estate trade magazine, but at the last minute she changed her mind and ended up tailoring her obit for the graduate newsletter of the small Midwestern college where she'd been a journalism major. Laura was amazed that her obituary not only pointed her right back to what she always thought she'd be doing, working as a reporter, but that she went even a step further and solidified a secret dream that she would end up right back in the Midwest as a professor at the college from which she'd graduated.

Until she did the professional obituary exercise, Laura hadn't discussed her desire to be a reporter or a professor, since her parents had vehemently shot down both career options as nonlucrative and unfulfilling and she had abandoned those goals. The exercise enabled her to tap into her creative spirit, which then revealed her true passions. She now began to see her future in a new light. Whether or not she followed the path mapped out in the obituary wasn't the point. It was now clear to her what she didn't want to do—sell real estate. The creative exercise of writing the obituary also made it clear to Laura that her "quarter-century crisis" had to do with her having made her decisions based on other people's feelings instead of her own. As much as she'd wracked her conscious brain over these issues, her rational mind couldn't seem to get to the underlying emotions. As Laura discovered, sometimes the best way to the pragmatic self is through the creative self.

SUMMARY: COMMIT TO THE MOVEMENT

My favorite dance teacher in college used to tell us to "commit to the movement." What she meant by that was no matter how you interpreted the moves, or whether or not you nailed the choreography, you had to commit to the movement and dance it fully. That was the only way to tell if your body was positioned properly or if you were executing the dance steps and the timing with precision and accuracy. If you made a wishy-washy, half-hearted attempt, she couldn't tell if you needed further instruction or not. Better to let the creative spirit take over, get out of the way of your own fears about the outcome, and commit to dancing boldly, if occasionally badly.

In chapter ten, we tapped into our intuitive spirit, deepening the trust in our own instincts as we learned to take our creative expressions into the outside world. By unlocking your creative spirit with artistic endeavors like starting a dream diary or painting a masterpiece, we let the mind free-flow instead of staying stuck in an analytical rut. And by learning to cash in on your passion, we can start to brain-storm about creative ways to approach our careers as well as our lives.

In the next chapter, one step at a time, we'll tackle the first draft of your Traveling Hopefully Personal Road map. So open your creative mind, commit to the movement, and let's turn your passions, dreams and goals into a step-by-step road map for success.

11

One Step at a Time

Creating Your Traveling Hopefully
Personal Road Map

"Action is eloquence."
—William Shakespeare

There is a beautiful old quilt mounted on a rough-hewn hunk of crown molding hanging on a wall in my Hollywood office. The quilt, which used to live at the foot of my bed, is there for two reasons. Since my company is headquartered on a union-affiliated studio lot, if I wanted my office painted, I would have to hire union workers to come in during their off hours, paying them overtime for their services. Although I care about esthetics, the sheer costs involved offend my thrift-store sensibilities so I use my quilt to mask my stark white wall. The second, and more significant, reason is that the quilt is a constant visual reminder of the delicate complexity of life. As I write or talk on the phone, I love to look at the intricate interlaced circular patterns to see if I can follow one line of colorful loops from the curvy scalloped edges to the center of the quilt where all the circles finally converge.

In this chapter, we're going to connect the big chunks of color as well as the little loose ends of your life and interweave them into a personal road map that is both practical and pleasing, like a quilt. The Fourth Step to Jumpstart Your Life, your road map will bring into laser focus your plan to manifest the vision you've created in the past ten chapters, bursting with beauty, power, and richness. First, like the stitching on the underside of my quilt, which faces the wall rather than the world, you will have to craft the knots and seams to hold it all in place.

By the time you have completed this chapter, you'll have a detailed, custom blueprint for life transformation—your Traveling Hopefully Personal Road map—which you can begin to implement today. If you take immediate positive action, I guarantee you will see immediate positive results. The only mistake you can make as you travel hopefully is to be unwilling to make a mistake. So don't worry about wrong turns or blunders as you proceed—and dare to be brilliant!

DEFINING YOUR LIFE OF PURPOSE AND PASSION

Can you describe the life you want to lead? In a moment, I'm going to ask you sum up your vision of your best possible life in a short paragraph or two. I know it's a tall order, but you've already done the legwork. Now, it's just a matter of getting a solid working definition down on paper. In order to give you a clear sense of what I'm talking about, the following is my definition of a life of purpose and passion. It's what I continually refer to as my benchmark for my best life when I'm making decisions about the people or projects I invite into my life and how I will spend the hours in my day. Gauging my commitments against my definition of a purposeful life is how I determine if I'm traveling toward my vision or moving away from it.

My definition of my best life of purpose and passion:

My definition of a life of purpose and passion is to live at the intersection of my personal passions and professional goals. Specifically, that means running my own communications company dedicated to nurturing, healing, and guiding others; using both my creative and analytical selves; and working with people whom I like, trust, and respect on projects that I care about. My business, in addition to challenging and satisfying me, must sustain a level of financial success that allows me the freedom and resources to devote generous amounts of love, time, and energy to my children, friends, and ultimately, I hope, a romantic partner. Physical fitness; spiritual and intellectual growth; and fun and adventure are key elements in my personal pursuits, which must blend and balance with my professional life.

The fact that other people might criticize what I look for in life as being touchy-feely, New Age, or noncommercial is irrelevant to me. They may think that concepts like passion are fine for home or place of worship, but not in their everyday lives and certainly not at work. Of course, everyone is entitled to his own beliefs; that's the whole point of having a personal definition. As far as I am concerned, passion and purpose, along with a sense of hopefulness, are the qualities I most desire to bring to every aspect of my life—at work, at home, with my kids and friends. This is what I want for my life, and if I can make it work, that's all I care about. If not, then at least I can use my goals as my standard for determining what is not working and how I can fix it. Choose your words carefully as you craft your definition of your best possible life so that it reflects who you are and honors who you want to become as you travel hopefully.

It is important that your goals be expansive enough to cover all aspects of your life and to grow as you grow, but to be specific enough that you can hold yourself accountable. If your description of your best possible life isn't a vital tool in helping you make decisions, then you're making it much more difficult to travel hopefully toward the life you've painstakingly envisioned. Take a look at my description again, then the questions below, and you'll see what I mean. When I am deciding if should take on a new client, project, or pursuit in either my professional or personal life, I ask myself specific questions that help to hold me accountable to achieving the life I want, including:

- Will this project allow me to nurture, heal, or guide others?
- Will I be devoting my time and energy to people whom I like, trust, and respect?
- Will a potential professional pursuit take too much precious personal time from my children and friends?
- Will the recreation, sport, or hobby I'm considering bring me a sense of fun, adventure, or physical well-being?
- Does this endeavor or relationship move me toward what I want and away from what no longer serves me?

It's your turn. Write out your specific yet expansive description of your best life of purpose and passion in your

Traveling Hopefully Daybook. Now, take a few projects or relationships you're considering, or have recently considered, bringing into your life. Put them to the test, even if by hindsight, by asking yourself questions based on your view of your best possible life. See if your answers help to hold you accountable.

Amy, a thirty-two-year-old Internet marketing consultant living in Atlanta, approached me to coach her through a major transition. Until recently, Amy had been a midlevel manager for a large technology firm, but her company shut down her department and outsourced their services. The good news for Amy was that her employers asked her to continue to consult part-time for them. Simultaneously, Amy hoped to build a home-based business that would eventually be her full-time career. One of her primary goals in working at home was to spend more time with her eight-year-old son. Amy came to me because she knew that I specialized in helping people shift from the corporate to the entrepreneurial world and that I had two kids and a somewhat unconventional, but very satisfying, family structure.

At first, what Amy wanted sounded straightforward, but as we began to peel back the onion layers of her life, it was clear that there was much more to her story than had initially met the eye. Amy had married young and within two years gave birth to her son. Three years later, her former college sweetheart husband died in a freak accident on a job site. Amy was devastated by her husband's death and convinced that, if not for her son, she might never have recovered from her grief. But she did recover, one day at a time, and after five years of merely surviving, decided she was ready to create a better life for herself and her son.

As I have witnessed again and again, once you make a conscious declaration to move your life in a more positive direction—even if you merely whisper it to the universe—events and people conspire to help you. Just as Amy was debating whether she could afford to start her business and hire me to guide her, she received a windfall settlement related to her husband's death that she had long since abandoned hope of ever receiving. The settlement, as well as the part-time account from her former company, was just enough of a financial cushion to give her the confidence that she could move toward becoming an entrepreneur. As we began to work together, it became clear that becoming an entrepreneur was just one small part of her big picture vision. Amy wasn't just setting up a new business; she was setting up a new life.

Amy's situation as a widowed, single mother in the throes of career change was dramatic and challenging, but the process she used to design her personal road map was the same as the one I'm sharing with you and that I'd recommend to anyone. Even if your circumstances are far less emotionally charged or painful, designing your road map still requires that you follow the same steps Amy did to plan her life transformation. I've used Amy's story as an example throughout this chapter, because she faced major obstacles and yet made sweeping changes in nearly every aspect of her life. I hope you'll agree that Amy's success is both instructional and inspirational.

Of course, when she was in the midst of all these personal and professional changes, Amy, like anyone, often felt frustrated and alone. As one of the first recruits in Amy's Support Squad—a concept she immediately embraced and employed—it was my job to challenge and support her on her journey. Amy had to learn to solicit support for her uphill climb, just like the group of girls I described who were scaling the sand dune in Manhattan Beach and cheering each other all the way to the top. One of the most important things I could do for her was to remind her not just to keep her eye on the summit but to look back down the hill occasionally to see how far she had already climbed. I encourage you to do the same as you design your Traveling Hopefully Personal Road map. Of course, if you haven't actually climbed the dune, even partway, by doing the necessary homework laid out in the first ten chapters of this book, this chapter won't hold much meaning for you. Don't shortchange yourself or your prospects for life change. If you haven't already done so, go back through the Hopeful Tools we've covered so far so that these concepts will work for you when we weave them all together.

To kick off Amy's hopeful and life changing journey, I explained the Five Steps to Jumpstart Your Life and the 21 Hopeful Tools. She balked a bit at the thought of looking at her overall life plan, since she was certain all she needed was a little business direction. When she finally acknowledged how intertwined her business and family lives were, she realized she couldn't overhaul one without affecting the other. Ultimately, she was glad she reconsidered and dealt with her transformation as a whole-life process. We started at the beginning, with Amy's vision of what her best life of purpose and passion would look like to her, which focused on starting her new business.

Granted, there were big chunks of Amy's social, romantic, and physical life that she had not yet addressed, but her initial big picture definition for her career change was a great start. From there, we began to break down that vision into bottom line action steps as we worked through the Five Steps to Jumpstart Your Life.

Amy's Definition of a Life of Purpose and Passion:

My life of purpose and passion would consist of my working a thirty- to forty-hour work-week, with a part-time housekeeper to cook, clean, and watch Steven while I'm finishing my day. I would consult from my home office on a variety of Internet projects that were either interesting or profitable (or both!), but I'd still have time to volunteer at Steven's school one morning a week and to get both of us involved in church and church-related activities again.

As we proceed with designing your road map, I'll refer back to some of the 21 Hopeful Tools, highlighting the ones that best translate directly into actionable and measurable items. Please note that I am not asking you to reinvent the wheel here. If you think you've accurately answered a particular question before, just sum up your answer again. If you think you were close the first time you encountered the tool or question but could benefit from revisiting a particular tool, here's your chance to refine your answer further.

Since we are creating a custom action map, specific to your needs, anytime there is a tool or exercise other than the one I've specified that you wish to review or substitute as part of your process, by all means, do so. I've had clients who visited their healing sanctuary daily, others who adhered to their list of 3 P's religiously. If you've made it this far, you certainly know which tools resonate for you, so don't hesitate to use them. It's time to get out your Traveling Hopefully Daybook or a notebook, follow the process along with Amy, and begin to record your reactions in preparation for creating your personal road map.

REFINING YOUR DESCRIPTION OF A LIFE OF PURPOSE AND PASSION

Once Amy had a solid working definition of her best possible life, understanding that it was always subject to change at her discretion, we began to refine that definition by using the Five Steps to Jumpstart Your Life as groundwork for her written road map. I'll share some of Amy's answers as we go, while you're fashioning your own. Then we'll put hers together at the end of this chapter in Amy's personal road map which you will use as a model for yours. Here goes!

STEP ONE: Dissect Your Past, So You Can Direct Your Future

1. In one or two sentences each, describe the negative recurring life themes you are living as a result of your family legacies. Now, move from accepting these negative life themes passively to overcoming them by stating specifically how you would rewrite those themes to be more positive.

2. Unload your family baggage by identifying the three most significant tags your family gave you. If they are negative, use your flip-side logic to rewrite them as more positive tags. If they are positive, rewrite them as positive action steps.

Amy's Response to Step One:

1. I never trust my own judgment because my parents made all my decisions for me. It is time to step up to the plate and live my own life, whether my family understands and supports me or not. I will make sure that the action steps outlined in my road map are bold and decisive!

2. My family tagged me "Baby" because I was the baby of the family. This also implied that I was incompetent and helpless. I will flip that tag over to read "Loved and Loving." My other family tag that I have long since outgrown, though no

one knows it but me, is "Princess," because my family viewed me as spoiled and fussy and needing constant care. Not true. "Princess" has now become "Power Player."

Do you hear Amy's underlying family theme? Even though she'd been in the workplace most of her adult life and sole support of herself and her child for the past five years, she'd nonetheless hung on to this outdated image of herself as the incompetent, needing-to-be-cared-for baby of the family. As she planned to launch a business and rebuild her life, she needed to stay strong and be willing to commit to taking bold action. Identifying those outdated life themes and committing to overcoming them helped steer Amy toward powerful people and purposeful actions.

Look over your responses to step one and see if you can identify the themes you want to avoid as you craft your road map. By dissecting your past, you'll get a good sense of how to shore up your weaknesses as you build on your strengths.

STEP TWO: Link Internal Clarity with External Action

This step may be the most important lesson I can ever share with you. Internal clarity is a sense of awareness that can help you turn down the volume on all the noise in your life so you can hear your own inner guidance. It's what some refer to as the still, small voice, or your inner wisdom, or even the voice of God or hand of the universe. Once you understand how to tap into that internal voice, which I've described in numerous exercises throughout this book, you can form a crystal-clear vision of the kind of life you want. Go back to the following Hopeful Tools for further clarification about building your inner vision through internal clarity: envisioning your healing sanctuary; meeting your future self, creating a personal credo;

is your life a fairy tale, a legend, or a myth?; reinvent yourself through verbal meditation; naming and taming your inner voices.

Forming the internal vision is only half the battle. Once you have a keen inner sense of what you want in your life, then you can translate that internal vision into external action. Not surprisingly, most people are more adept at one or the other. Some people have no problem tapping into their internal wisdom, but they fail to then act upon the guidance they receive. Others are in constant motion, but they take action for action's sake rather than navigating toward a predetermined destination. We'll deal with more of the specifics of external action as we create your road map.

When you combine internal clarity with external action magic happens. The powerful combination of clarity and action is unstoppable. It's important for you to have a sense of where you fall on the internal/external continuum so that you can anticipate where you need help in linking the inner with the outer. Take a moment now to refer back to the internal dreamer or external doer test you took in chapter three. Where did you fall on the dreamer/doer continuum?

Amy's score of thirty-six put her in the "Balanced: Dreamer Who Does" category. Somewhat more introspective than action-oriented, Amy knew that if she was going to make the dramatic life changes she envisioned, she would have to counteract the "baby of the family" theme with a strong commitment to living her best possible life. It was time to call for reinforcements, namely Amy's Support Squad.

STEP THREE: Recruit a Support Squad

Now that you—along with Amy—have identified specific goals that you want to meet within the next year, you're probably beginning to see how having the appropriate support and guidance can really shorten your growth curve. Maybe you can figure it all out yourself. But why should you? Especially when your Support Squad is out there just waiting to be recruited.

Take a look back at your goals from your 3 P's exercise and mark off every item with which you'd like some outside help. Right now we're concerned with broad overall goals. We'll be breaking them down into specific action steps in a minute. Don't be concerned with whether help should come from a paid professional or a personal favor. Just identify the items for which you need help. Next, look at any of the items you think you could probably accomplish on your own, but which might be hastened with some outside counsel. Again, this help might come from paid professionals or personal favors and could be in the form of hard data, strategic market intelligence, financial information, emotional support, and physical training. If you're like me, you went into this exercise thinking you might need a little help here or there with the tough stuff like taxes or plumbing. But the truth is, once you really examine your list, there are so many things that your army can help you with—once you've recruited them, that is.

Look down your list of goals and in another column alongside, write out a list of potential recruits for your Support Squad. If you know the person, write his or her name next to the goal you'd like that person's help with. If you know the function, but not the person, write out the type of function next to the goal; for example, "personal trainer," "general contractor," etc. Identifying the function is the first step toward finding the person. If you have a person who would make a great addition to your squad, but you're unsure what their role might be, record their names as free agents and figure out their roles later.

As you envision the recruiting process, remember the two-step conversation:

- Concisely state your goal with specifics about how your potential Support Squad member might aid you in your process.
- Graciously—and immediately—let your recruit off the hook by acknowledging that you understand if they do not have the time or resources to help you and request that they refer you to someone who might.

Make sure that the support and guidance your Support Squad can give you aligns as closely as possible with your goals, but don't overlook a great recruit just because you're not sure what role he or she might play on your traveling hopefully journey. I give people great points for passion and generosity. Just their willingness to be on your team can mean a great deal, you can figure out their exact role later.

Finally, I cannot overstate the importance of giving support and guidance in return. If someone agrees to help you meet your goals, you are beholden to return the favor as aggressively as you possibly can. If you happen to have a Support Squad of high-functioning folks who don't really need anything in return, offer assistance to their family members, colleagues, old roommates from out of town—anything you can do to return the favor, particularly if they are giving you unpaid personal guidance or support. It's just good manners to give back.

Amy's Support Squad:

Amy had had a large network of friends and colleagues in her community, but since she'd become widowed, she found it extremely awkward to socialize or to take advantage of offers as diverse as babysitting Steven or introducing her to potential business prospects. Now that she was traveling hopefully toward getting her life back on track, she knew it was time to start recruiting her Support Squad. Taking her list of goals, Amy matched up people and their potential contributions with nearly every item on her list!

Amy checked out her church, former company, networking associations, friends, neighbors, Steven's school, and professional organizations to round out her army. After she had recruited everyone she felt she needed to jumpstart her new business, she decided she would begin a one-on-one brainstorming process with each of them. Then she threw an old-fashioned backyard pot-luck, inviting friends and family members—as well as her Support Squad—to celebrate.

AMY'S SUPPORT SQUAD:

Old boss—business and financial guidance

President of local small business owners' organization—business and networking help

Attorney—legal/business

CPA—financial guidance for business/college fund/retirement accounts

Pastor—spiritual guidance

Choir director—emotional and vocal help (joining the choir again!)

Trainer from the Y—physical support and de-stressing teacher

Steven's teacher and school counselor—parental and educational help

Beloved housekeeper/sitter for Steven (like member of family)

Two best friends—emotional support!

Handyman/builder (my single guy neighbor—he fixes, I cook)

STEP FOUR: Creating Your Traveling Hopefully Personal Road map

This is where we begin to translate the internal vision into concrete external action. If you need a reminder about how to begin this process, go back to chapter eight and take another look at your reactions to discovering the power of the 3 P's and taking the timeline test. If you haven't completed those two tools yet, do them right now. They are the building blocks of your road map and it will be impossible to proceed without them.

Look at your 3 P's list in which you've identified and stated your goals with regard to your profession, personal life, and the possessions you wish to own. Next, look at the accompanying timeline you created to coincide with those goals. Right now, condense that list down to just the 3 P's goals that had a "within one year" on the timeline. We're going to focus your road map on these one-year personal, professional, and possession goals. Don't worry if something you care about doesn't make the one-year cut; you can always reprioritize later and move items up the list as you start to cross off items you've already accomplished.

Amy's Response to Step Four:

PROFESSIONAL

Maintain/grow account with former employer	1 Year
Bring in two new freelance accounts	1 Year
Increase earnings	1 Year
Join two professional organizations	1 Year
Start networking	1 Year

PERSONAL

Volunteer at Steven's school	1 Year
Join a gym	1 Year
Get active in church with Steven	1 Year
Cook dinner three times a week	1 Year
Have a Christmas party	1 Year

POSSESSIONS

Start Steven's college fund	1 Year
Redo Steven's "big kid" bedroom	1 Year
Buy good home office equipment	1 Year
Remodel bathroom	1 Year

Now we'll begin to put the layers one on top of the next in the first draft of Amy's road map. Only now we're breaking down her big-picture goals into specific action steps. When you've finished reading through Amy's road map, it will be time to create yours in Hopeful Tool #21.

AMY'S TRAVELING HOPEFULLY PERSONAL
ROAD MAP

Amy's Life of Purpose and Passion

- My life or purpose and passion would include my working a thirty- to forty-hour work-week, with a part-time housekeeper to cook, clean, and watch Steven while I'm finishing my day. I would consult from my home office on a variety of Internet projects that were either interesting or profitable (or both!), but I'd still have time to volunteer at Steven's school one morning a week and to get both of us involved in church and church-related activities again.

Goals, Action Steps and Timetable

Maintain/grow account with former employer

- Dedicate 20–30 hours per week to account—within one week
- In-person meeting with client on weekly basis—within one week
- Get college intern to assist me—within one month
- Support Squad member: Former boss

Bring in two new freelance accounts

- Get referrals from former boss—within two weeks
- Build marketing presence online—within three months
- Take out ad in tech trade journals—within three months
- Support Squad members: Old boss, best friends, networking organization contacts

Increase earnings

- Create business/financial plan—within one month
- Set sales targets—within one month
- Support Squad members: Old boss, attorney, CPA

Join two professional organizations

- Join women in business organization—within six months
- Attend church group for local business people—within three months
- Support Squad members: President of women's business association, best friend, pastor

Volunteer at Steven's school

- Sign up for reading group assistant—within two weeks

- Volunteer for carnival—within two months
- Determine additional opportunities for year-round involvement—within two weeks
- Support Squad member: Steven's teacher

Join a gym

- Go to aerobics class at church (free!)—within two months
- Get short-term trainer with gym membership—within four months
- Support Squad members: Trainer, best friends

Get active in church with Steven

- Attend service weekly—within one week
- Go to after-service function—within one month
- Rejoin choir—within three months
- Support Squad members: Pastor, choir director

Cook dinner three times a week

- Just do it! (okay, keep checklist on fridge)—within one day
- Cook with Steven at least once a week—within one week
- Have friends/family over for weekend lunch or dinner—within one week
- Support Squad member: Housekeeper

Have a Christmas party

- Plan with Steven and Grandma—within two weeks
- Send out invitations by November 15 (then I can't chicken out!)—within two months
- Support Squad members: Best friends, housekeeper

Start Steven's college fund

- Get educated on different funds — within one month
- Research costs of college — within three months
- Get Steven involved — chores for contributions — within one month
- Support Squad members: Steven's teacher, CPA

Redo Steven's "big kid" bedroom/remodel bathroom

- Work out a deal with my neighbor — within six months
- Steven and I can start pulling pix out of magazines — within two months
- Support Squad members: Neighbor/handyman

Buy good home office equipment

- Upgrade computer — within one month
- Purchase new computer — within six months
- Review business plan and equipment needs — within six months
- Support Squad members: Old boss, CPA

Amy's process of defining her big-picture vision and translating that into bottom-line action immediately took her to a much more hopeful place than she'd been in many years. Although at first Amy expected this process simply to produce a business plan, by the time she completed her Traveling Hopefully Personal Road map — and had barely begun implementing it — she was already spending more recreational time with her son, investing in a spiritual life, building a financial future, even starting to cook and sing again. All while she launched a business. Talk about locating the intersection between personal passions and professional pursuits!

Tool # 21: Creating a Traveling Hopefully Personal Road map

Now it's your turn to create the first draft of your personal road map. Remember this is a work in progress, a living document always subject to change. In your daybook, structure your road map based on the key elements listed below. Refer to Amy's road map if you need clarification as you design your own.

- Write out your description of your life of purpose and passion.
- List your one-year 3 P's goals, then break each item down into two to four specific action steps, that is, precisely defined and measurable steps to which you can hold yourself accountable. Put each action step to the timeline test in terms of months or weeks, within the overall one-year time frame. Look at Amy's goals and action steps below to see how she included specific measurements to know when she had reached her stated goals as well as different methods she used to help herself be accountable to each goal/action step.
- Draft your Support Squad, first on paper, then in real life. List by name and/or function, attaching at least one to a specific goal.
- Take action on at least one of your goals within twenty-four hours. Celebrate your success!

Congratulations! You're on your way, traveling hopefully with your personal road map to guide you. The next step as well as the final chapter will help you unleash the power of perseverance.

STEP FIVE: Move Toward What You Want and Away from What No Longer Serves You

In Chapter Twelve, our final chapter, we'll discuss the Fifth Step to Jumpstart Your Life—moving toward what you want and away from what no longer serves you. Without this critical element of perseverance, all the passion and planning in the world won't amount to a thing. But all winners know that passion and planning—combined with perseverance—will get you over the finish line every time!

STEPPING STONES

When my ex-husband and I made the difficult decision that we needed to end our marriage, we decided the best thing we could do for our children was to establish two separate households where the boys would be comfortable and feel at home. My requirements for that second home were that it be less than ten minutes away from my ex-husband's, that each boy would have his own room, and that the new house, like the old one, would have a big backyard.

I found that home, a lovely 1940s California cottage in a quiet middle-class neighborhood about eight minutes from my ex-husband's house. It wasn't a Beverly Hills mansion or a Malibu beachfront estate, but it was home. I was happier there than I'd been in a long time. When one of my entertainment clients asked me where I lived, I told him about my little neighborhood. He expressed in no uncertain terms his shock that I could live in such an "unchic location." Later, when the kids and I landscaped the front yard, planting ornamental plum trees and hedges of rosemary, we placed a little walkway of old worn stepping stones from the curb to the purple-hued front door, and I reflected on just

how chic it was to enjoy my home and my boys. Besides being rude, what my client had clearly missed was that the
purchase of my home was based on my definition of my best
possible life — not his — and that having a lovely house with
a big backyard in a modest neighborhood eight minutes
from my kids' dad represented the perfect real estate scenario to me.

In designing your own personal road map you have discovered the power of creating a custom definition of your
most passionate and purposeful life and refining that definition into goals and measurable action steps. You have sam-
pled other people's struggles and success stories along the
way, including mine and, I hope, learned from both. Now it is
time for you to start living your Traveling Hopefully Personal
Road map.

SUMMARY: IT'S YOUR TRIPLE AXLE

A figure skater who blew a critical jump, ruining a make-
or-break routine in a key skating competition, was interviewed by a sportscaster afterward and pointedly asked
what went wrong. I've long since forgotten who the skater
was, but I'll never forget the response. The skater said, "I
didn't stay inside my triple axle." Meaning? She lost control at a critical moment, and blew the jump, as well as the
championship.

Clearly, that skater had passion. What else would get her
on the ice for five hours a day of practice? She had a carefully
planned and artfully choreographed routine that was meant
to get her to the championship. And, just as you'll have, she
experienced a setback. Disappointing? Yes. Humiliating?
Maybe. The end of her skating career? Absolutely not.

As we'll learn in chapter twelve, passion and planning are

only two thirds of getting you where you want to go. Possibly the most critical element of all is perseverance. That's the essence of the Fifth Step to Jumpstart Your Life: Keep moving toward what you want and away from what no longer serves you. In other words, refuse to give up, persevere. Stay inside your triple axle no matter what the world throws at you. Just like that skater, who I'll guarantee was back out on the ice the very next day.

12

Staying the Course

Passion, Planning, and Perseverance

"If we are facing in the right direction,
all we have to do is keep on walking."

—Buddhist proverb

I am a sucker for movies about underdogs. Whether it's *Rocky, Seabiscuit,* or the runners in *Chariots of Fire,* nothing delights me more than seeing the underdogs come out from behind and win big. In each of those stories, fervent passion and an aggressive plan of attack are the common elements that get the heroes halfway home. Who can forget Sylvester Stallone's classic portrayal of Rocky claiming the streets and meat-packing plants of Philadelphia as his personal training ground? Talk about combining unflagging passion with aggressive and original action planning. But even beyond the critical elements of passion and planning, what gets those protagonists to the finish line every time is perseverance.

Plain and simple, perseverance is the refusal to give up, despite whatever delays, backsliding, or setbacks life throws at you. In our final chapter, we're going to talk about the Fifth Step to Jumpstart Your Life, which is to keep moving toward what you want and away from what no longer serves you. After all, now that you've completed the 21 Hopeful Tools, you've already done the hard work of creating an internal vision of your best possible life of purpose and passion. You've designed a specific and measurable road map to begin to create that life in the external world. Now all we have to do is ensure that you'll keep moving forward on your well-crafted path. So what will keep you moving forward, you're asking? What's going to separate you from all the other people in the world with the same wonderful intentions of redefining their careers, overhauling their fitness plans, or improving their relationships? What makes you so special? You understand the nature of perseverance and you know the 21 tips and tactics that keep you moving toward your vision. That is, you will by the time you finish this chapter.

First we're going to explore three key concepts related to perseverance and its importance to keeping you on your path. They are:

- Setting hopeful but realistic expectations
- Leveraging your current situation
- Letting your roads converge

Then I'll outline 21 tips and tactics to keep you on the path of perseverance, as you move toward your big-picture goal and away from what you've decided to leave far behind. You will have already encountered some of these tactics in earlier chapters, but now they will serve as timely reminders to keep you from backsliding as you learn to make success a habit.

SET HOPEFUL BUT REALISTIC EXPECTATIONS

With tools like the 3 P's exercise and the personal road map, you've set some very specific goals, many of which already have well-defined timetables and measurable outcomes. Now, as you begin to implement the action steps within your road map, you'll need to make ongoing changes and course corrections. It's just part of the process of Traveling Hopefully and jump-starting change in the real world, in practice and not in theory. As you increase the number and degree of the risks you're starting to take, you will need to regularly reassess your own expectations by challenging your definition of success, as well as the goals you've set and the time frames you've established.

I don't want to burst your bubble, but I will warn you right now that life change takes time. I always let my clients who are in transition know that however long they've allotted to make the life changes they're seeking, they need to double it. At least. But think about it, if you're really committed to overhauling your life, isn't it worth investing the time and energy? It's essential that you manage your own expectations and take an internal reality check on what is possible and how long it might take. Keep your goals and expectations of yourself as aggressive and ambitious as you can handle, but be aware when you're striving too hard. If you need a little more clarity on whether or not you're being realistic in your goal-setting, action planning, or your overall expectations of yourself, step back and take in the broad view. Review your Traveling Hopefully Daybook to detect any areas in which your written expectations are out of synch with what feels right to you now. Tune in to your inner voices to hear points of view and perspectives about your progress.

If you need some external insight, check in with your Support Squad, trusted friends, or family members so that you don't build unrealistic goals and give up out of frustration. Don't cut yourself too much slack if what you need is a firm nudge in the right direction, but conversely, don't push yourself too fast or too hard if you really need a break. Pay attention to your emotions as well as your actions. If you fail to set your expectations realistically, you're only setting yourself up for failure. And that's the last thing we want. In order to persevere, you need to acknowledge if not celebrate success—any success—along the way.

Marlena was a twenty-four-year-old yoga instructor. She was very attractive, smart, and talented, and all she could ever remember wanting to be was a rock star. Marlena had enormous talent, but she had set up extremely unrealistic expectations about how quickly she could get a manager to represent her, a producer to cut her first demo, and a label to sign her to a recording contract. She came to me beaten down and broken-hearted over the career she was sure she'd already lost.

The truth was, in a very short time Marlena had made significant progress. But her well-received showcase performances and her ever-improving songwriting skills didn't even register as successes to her because she inaccurately assumed she could go from yoga teacher to rock star within a year. I'm sure that could happen for some lucky soul, but it certainly wasn't typical and it hadn't happened for Marlena. Creating a professional infrastructure and getting on the record companies' radar in less than twelve months was a pretty tall order for a kid from Sioux City, Iowa. Eventually, Marlena was able to reassess her expectations and acknowledge the success she'd already experienced. With hope and confidence restored, Marlena was able to identify new, realistic goals and deadlines with which to mark her progress so she could keep moving toward her vision.

LEVERAGE YOUR CURRENT SITUATION

I don't advocate sweeping overnight change. It's great if you get caught up in the momentum of life transformation, but it shouldn't be at the expense of your children, spouse, or job. There's a reason that many successful support organizations tell their members not to make any big changes within a year of recognizing their addiction or other problem. Sometimes you can move toward your goals much more quickly by using your current environment than by abandoning it. As you make the necessary internal changes, you can take external action right in your current situation. You can think of this concept in terms of leveraging your current situation in your personal life, for example by learning new skills in a relationship even though you recognize that it may not be lasting. This isn't meant to be a form of manipulation, merely a recognition that short-term or impermanent situations can be positive learning experiences. But let's think of this concept in terms of your professional life, what I generally call leveraging your day job.

Ann worked at a large software company as a project manager for various clients. She loved the work, but had always thought she'd start her own Web business by the time she was thirty. Now thirty-two, Ann came to me because she knew I had successfully segued from the corporate to the entrepreneurial world.

After I became a serial career changer, I began to coach people through difficult or nontraditional corporate-to-corporate or corporate-to-entrepreneurial transitions. I always discouraged them from quitting their day jobs prematurely, just as I did Ann. Even if you've decided that you are in the wrong line of work, that you're just not cut out to be a nine-to-fiver, or that you have a burning itch to jump headlong into your new passion, don't forget the practical obligations you have.

Remember, too, that rather than burning bridges, you might actually be able to travel across them on your way to where you want to go, possibly even taking support or allies with you.

Your day job, even if you're dissatisfied with it, can be ripe with opportunities to learn new skills and make new contacts. Once you've decided where you're headed, you can successfully leverage your day job by taking on relevant projects, volunteering for committees, or beginning to recruit your Support Squad. And you often do so from a much stronger position within an existing company than you do as your own start-up or in a new position where you need to focus on proving your value. So don't throw out the baby with the bath water. Instead, begin to think of yourself as your own independent company, even when you're working for another company. Start racking up new skills in the areas of finance, marketing, sales—whatever you're going to need to get your best possible life off the ground.

When Ann realized that she could leverage her day job and begin to build the sort of heavyweight connections she'd need when she started her own business, she was able to see her job in an entirely new light. Now she went after high-level projects and clients much more forcefully—because it was part of her big-picture vision—and she discovered that she was enjoying her job much more as a result of some of the new assignments she was able to land. She adjusted her expectations and reset her timeline. With a renewed sense of purpose, Ann was able to leverage her day job and persevere toward what she wanted and away from what no longer served her.

LET YOUR ROADS CONVERGE

Have you ever heard the beautiful Robert Frost poem "The Road Not Taken"? It speaks of a place where "two roads diverged in a yellow wood" and a traveler who could have chosen either path but decided to walk the road that was "grassy and wanted wear." Rather than pick the obviously more traveled path, he continues his journey on the road less traveled and anticipates that one day he will be telling the story of how that simple choice made all the difference. Frost's implication, of course, is that while most people automatically make the safer choices in life, there are some brave souls who are willing to take the riskier road and are the better for it.

Think about those two roads for a moment. One path is the status quo—your current job, relationships, all the different aspects of your life that we've been discussing in terms of family baggage and negative themes. That path is limiting and restrictive and offers little joy or meaning. That is the path you know all too well because you're currently walking it.

Now, think about all the work you've done to envision your best possible life of purpose and passion. Imagine that life of clear internal vision and bold external action as a second path. Picture that beautiful yellow wood which Robert Frost so poignantly describes. Only now instead of having to choose one road over the other, you can have both as they come together somewhere in the woods—the life you've lived up until now and the life you want and deserve. See your roads converging until the life you led becomes the life you lead. Don't think of the path behind you as wasted time or motion. Whatever you had to go through, it has brought you to this yellow wood. Let your roads converge, so that when you leave the woods you will leave the old path behind and walk out on your new path. That is the essence of the Fifth Step to Jumpstart Your Life.

As you persevere down your new path, maybe people will notice as you start to write a column in your company newsletter, lose weight and update your image, start your own business, tackle a new hobby or relationship. Or maybe they won't discover anything new about you until your entire life has transformed right under their noses and suddenly the ugly duckling has become a swan. Just keep those two roads firmly in mind and when you feel you are backsliding or losing ground, picture the path you really want to travel.

Cynthia and Kevin were a long-married husband and wife who attended a workshop I led on jumpstarting life change. The fact that Cynthia and Kevin attended together spoke volumes about how committed they were to building better lives for themselves as individuals, but also as a couple. A major concern for Cynthia was that, despite all the progress she'd made to update her education and job skills so she could grow professionally, she was spending so much time on a job she'd long since outgrown that she couldn't seem to make much headway toward her new goals. Cynthia was torn between the desire to transform her life and guilt over rocking everyone else's boat. Kevin, who was completely supportive of his wife's goals, was at his wit's end since he'd suggested everything he could think of to get Cynthia to scale back her duties on her current job and start taking steps toward her future. Cynthia had no idea how to say no to her employers, even when she was certain she was being unfairly taken advantage of and had little opportunity for advancement.

When Cynthia began to work through the Hopeful Tools, recognizing the path she'd been on for many years as well as the path she wanted to travel, she began to envision the two coming together. Bit by bit, Cynthia found the courage to set some boundaries at her job, letting her employers know about her long-term educational and professional goals. With Kevin helping to hold her accountable, Cynthia cut back her work hours and enrolled in school. By the time she finished her two-year graduate program, she was working part-time for her old company while she interviewed for a new position more in line with her new career goals. Her perseverance paid off when she received a job offer with a significant salary increase in her new area of interest. Cynthia left her old road behind her, stepped onto her new path and never looked back.

21 TIPS AND TACTICS TO KEEP YOU ON THE PATH OF PERSEVERANCE

Perseverance requires that you understand that sometimes you need to cut yourself some slack, back off of your goals, and just take care of yourself. Other times you need to give yourself a swift kick in the rear to stay on track. You've built those vital self-assessment skills for a reason, so start using them. Remember that just like in nature, there is a rhythm, an ebb and flow, to our ability to change. You've got to learn to recognize when you need to do some pushing in order to move toward what serves you and when you need to let things flow unassisted.

Following are 21 tips and tactics to help you persevere toward your big-picture vision. Whenever you need some help, either by pulling back or ramping up, go through these tips and see which ones might work for you. As always, you can create new ones and start a list of your own in your Traveling Hopefully Daybook. Just keep one foot in front of the other and you'll make it!

1. Reach out and call a friend for encouragement.
2. Write out what you're feeling about your progress in your daybook.
3. Identify a specific action step you want to complete

and enlist a buddy or member of your Support Squad to stick with you until you've done it.

4. Offer to help someone else who's struggling with one of the same issues you are, whether it's fitness, parenting, or career problems.

5. Ask a few members of your Support Squad to get together to address a specific problem or issue about which each of them has information, expertise, or prior history. Be careful about mixing completely unrelated areas like your workout buddy and your career mentor.

6. Do some deep breathing exercises.

7. Enroll in an adult education or college course to help you meet one of your goals or learn a new skill.

8. Get your endorphins going and your body moving by taking a brisk walk or lifting some weights (even soup cans or water bottles).

9. Practice one of the visualization exercises like healing sanctuary.

10. Teach someone a skill that reinforces a step on your road map.

11. Do some uncensored brainstorming with a couple of pals around an issue where you feel stuck.

12. Pick a negative thought or action in which you habitually indulge and commit to stopping today. If you frequently tell yourself or others that you're fat, decide never to say that again and stick to it. Have your friends and family fine you if you break your rule.

13. Treat yourself to something that feels luxurious, even if it's only a supermarket bouquet or an inexpensive CD.

14. Explain one of the tools you've learned, like tapping into your creativity, to a child. Then indulge in whatever you've described.

15. Have a success party to celebrate having completed a small action step or an overall goal. Make sure it suits your budget and style, whether it's cake and coffee at

home or a fancy night on the town. Invite your genuine supporters to join you.

16. Become active in a cause or activity that renews your commitment to your own vision. If your vision includes a career change, join a group or class that strengthens that goal.

17. Find a new way to tout your successes. Start a family newsletter to brag about your recent accomplishments. Encourage everyone to join in and make some noise about their successes, too. Start a friends and family trend.

18. Deepen your faith. Whatever you believe spiritually, renew and expand your commitment. Join a church or temple, find a community of like-minded people, and find strength in numbers.

19. Take a break and back off your goals for a couple of days. Rather than kick yourself for slacking off or feeling guilty for not making progress, make a conscious decision that you're on holiday and enjoy the vacation.

20. Take Sundays off. There's a reason so many religious groups consider Sunday a day of rest. Try not working, not talking, not driving, or not watching TV one day a week and see how much more focus you can give yourself and your goals.

21. Take a risk. Large or small, try something you never thought you'd have the courage to do, whether it's making a speech at a Toastmaster's club, climbing a mountain, taking a ballroom dance class at the Y, or bungee jumping.

Perseverance isn't drudgery. It's a commitment to keep moving forward toward the vision you've created of your best possible life. You can do it—with passion, planning, and perseverance!

SUMMARY: LIVE TO THE POINT OF TEARS

On my last birthday, a friend of mine, who also happens to be a member of my Support Squad, sent me a card with a lovely Camus quote that said, "Live to the point of tears." It wasn't just the quotation, but her birthday note that touched me so deeply. She wrote, "You are my role model for courage, because you live life to the fullest."

Predictably, I burst into tears, proving the point that I lived not only to the point of tears but often beyond. I reflected on the message that had affected me so profoundly. My journey has not always been an easy one. I have shed many tears of frustration, loneliness, and sadness. Now, I shed tears of joy much more often. That is my hope for you.

As I travel my path, I never cease to be amazed that what I envision for myself, and often for others, comes to fruition in the real world. As I become more ambitious in my vision, the realities begin to heighten accordingly. From the sad, lonely little girl who firmly believed she was destined to live a life of joyless service and mind-numbing drudgery, devoid of love, I have transformed my life using the tools I share with you. I've created a highly satisfying business based on my personal passions, one I am able to operate on my own terms. My relationship with my children, my family, and my friends continues to grow deeper, richer, and more meaningful every day. My home and physical surroundings reflect my taste and are more comforting and pleasing than I once thought possible. As my spiritual life grows ever stronger, so does my physical body. To be sure, I have to reprioritize regularly, frequently calling upon my Support Squad, to maintain a healthy balance among all these passions in my life. I see that I can—and do—have the joyful life I seek, as long as I start with the vision, then do the work.

As the old saying goes, "People don't plan to fail, they fail to plan." I will not let that happen to you. That is my role as a member of your Support Squad. I am here to lead, inspire, and challenge you to begin your transformation. This is your call to action. You can have the life you want. Just think about how exciting it will be to begin your journey as you face new opportunities with excitement, enthusiasm, and hopefulness.

Just as my friend's note affirmed that I had made many positive transformations in my life, the Camus quote challenged me to consider what it means to "live to the point of tears" and whether I continued to do so as I traveled my path. I am dedicated to living my definition of joy and I pledge to be your partner in that process. I am committed to showing you that hope is eternal, support is available, and passion and purpose are yours for the asking. I congratulate you for finding the courage to create a new life and thank you for allowing me to be your partner as you travel hopefully on your journey.